AMERICA the BEAUTIFUL

WASHINGTON, D.C.

By Deborah Kent

Consultants

Kathryn Collison Ray, M.S., M.A., Assistant Chief, Washingtoniana Division,
Martin Luther King Memorial Library

Robert L. Hillerich, Ph.D., Bowling Green State University, Bowling Green, Ohio

CHILDRENS PRESS®
CHICAGO

Families enjoy one of the annual Easter egg hunts held on the White House lawn.

Project Editor: Joan Downing
Associate Editor: Shari Joffe
Design Director: Margrit Fiddle
Typesetting: Graphic Connections, Inc.
Engraving: Liberty Photoengraving

Library of Congress Cataloging-in-Publication Data

Kent, Deborah.
    America the beautiful. Washington, D.C./
by Deborah Kent.
        p.   cm.
    Summary: Discusses the geography, history,
people, government, economy, and recreation of
Washington, D.C.
    ISBN 0-516-00497-2
    1.   Washington (D.C.)—Juvenile literature.
[1.   Washington (D.C.)]
F194.3.K46   1990   90-35386
975.3—dc20   CIP
                                               AC

Georgian row houses
grace many of the streets
in historic Georgetown.

TABLE OF CONTENTS

Chapter 1

THE NATION'S BIGGEST COMPANY TOWN

THE NATION'S BIGGEST COMPANY TOWN

In hundreds of towns and cities across the United States, life revolves around the workings of a single corporation—a mining concern, a canning company, a steel manufacturer. In such communities, the majority of the people work for the company. Others provide goods and services for the company's workers. The company may have a strong influence in the town's government, and even in cultural and recreational programs.

The capital of the United States—Washington, the District of Columbia—is sometimes called "the nation's biggest company town." About 21 percent of the city's work force is employed within the vast web of offices, bureaus, agencies, and departments known as the federal government. Tens of thousands of other people provide the supplies that the government uses every day, as well as food, clothing, and housing for the government workers.

Each year, millions of visitors flock to Washington. They follow the streets where the giants of history have walked, gaze at the city's soaring spires and magnificent gilded domes, and explore its extraordinary museums and libraries. In awe, they enter the chambers of Congress and the Supreme Court, where decisions are made that map the world's future.

Like most American cities, Washington has seen strife and injustice as well as triumphs. Today, it is plagued by the same problems that beset most of the nation's urban centers. Yet its position as the capital of the United States makes Washington unique. It came into being because the nation's government needed a home, and for the past two centuries, the government has shaped its destiny.

Chapter 2
THE NATURAL SETTING

THE NATURAL SETTING

"I assure you that no position in America can be more susceptible of grand improvement than that between the Eastern Branch of the Potomac and Georgetown." So wrote French engineer Pierre-Charles L'Enfant in 1791, in boundless praise of the site that had been chosen for the capital of the newly formed United States.

GEOGRAPHY

The District of Columbia lies on the northern bank of the Potomac River. Covering 69 square miles (179 square kilometers), the city nestles between the Potomac River and the Anacostia. On a map, the city looks like a diamond-shaped nibble out of the state of Maryland's southern border. Virginia faces Washington across the Potomac to the south and west.

Some of Washington is built on the Atlantic Coastal Plain, a band of low-lying land that stretches from southern New Jersey to Florida. Rock Creek, in the city's northwestern section, marks the boundary with a more elevated geological region called the Piedmont. The Piedmont is a broad, fertile plateau that extends from Pennsylvania to Alabama.

Much of the area that is now Washington was once marshland, dense with underbrush and alive with ducks, herons, and other waterfowl. The flat land along the Anacostia River lies only a few

The waterfall at Pierce Mill, on Rock Creek

feet above sea level. The land rises to the west to form several low rounded hills. The most important of these is Jenkins Hill, better known as Capitol Hill, which stands 88 feet (27 meters) above sea level near the center of the city. The United States Capitol, the Library of Congress, and the Supreme Court all stand on Capitol Hill today.

RIVERS AND CREEKS

The Potomac River rises in the Blue Ridge Mountains at Maryland's westernmost tip, and empties into the broad finger of the Atlantic Ocean called Chesapeake Bay. As it reaches the Washington line, the river foams over the Little Falls. Below the falls, as it passes the western section of the city known as

The Tidal Basin is a large pool in West Potomac Park that was created as a flood-control measure.

Georgetown, the river tumbles between high, scenic bluffs, or palisades. When it descends to the Coastal Plain, however, the Potomac grows more sedate. By the time it reaches the mouth of the Anacostia, it is a placid, brackish stream nearly one mile (1.6 kilometers) wide.

As far west as Washington, the Potomac rises and falls with the Chesapeake's tides. During the early days of the capital, the river flooded frequently, causing serious property damage. As a flood-control measure, engineers created the Tidal Basin, a large pool in West Potomac Park.

Washington's smaller streams are all tributaries of the Potomac. The Anacostia meanders through low-lying, marshy land on the eastern edge of the city. Much of Constitution Avenue follows the course of Tiber Creek, which was covered over in the late nineteenth century. Rock Creek has carved out a narrow valley in the

Every spring, thousands of visitors come to Washington to see the Japanese cherry trees in bloom.

northwestern part of the city. Much of the valley remains wooded, preserved as the city's 1,800-acre (728-hectare) Rock Creek Park.

TREES, FLOWERS, AND WILDLIFE

Every spring, thousands of visitors flock to West Potomac Park to view the pink-and-white splendor of Japanese cherry blossoms around the Tidal Basin. Washington's Japanese cherry trees were donated as a gift of friendship by the mayor of Tokyo in 1912. Today, some 650 trees of two varieties bloom in West Potomac Park. Several other varieties grow in East Potomac Park, on an island in the river.

Arching over streets and avenues, trees enhance every section of the nation's capital. As early as 1805, when most Americans were concerned with cutting down forests to civilize the wilderness,

Virginia bluebells (left) and skunk cabbages (right) are among the wildflowers that bloom throughout Washington.

President Thomas Jefferson ordered the planting of Lombardy poplars along Pennsylvania Avenue. Many of the city's trees are "exotics," imported to the United States from other countries. These include Oriental ginkgos, ailanthus or trees of heaven, acacias, locusts, and Asiatic magnolias. Among the trees native to the area are sycamores, pin oaks, red oaks, American lindens, and willows. Most of the beautiful elm trees that once graced the city have fallen victim to Dutch elm disease, which swept the United States in the 1950s and 1960s.

Washington claims nearly 150 parks, and patches of wildflowers bloom throughout the city during the spring and summer months. As early as March, jack-in-the-pulpits and skunk cabbages can be found in the marshes around the Anacostia. By late April, golden groundsels and Virginia bluebells appear on higher ground. Trailing arbutus, bloodroots, and hepaticas grow on the ridges in Rock Creek Park.

The gray squirrels that thrive in Washington's parks have become expert panhandlers, begging fearlessly for peanuts from visitors. Raccoons, red foxes, opossums, muskrats, and flying squirrels survive in the more secluded sections of Rock Creek Park. Every spring, bird-watchers eagerly await the return of migrating warblers, thrushes, finches, and other songbirds that make the park their home. Mourning doves, chickadees, blue jays, and mockingbirds add color and music to the city's gardens and shade trees.

CLIMATE

Washington's winters are mild but damp, with an average January temperature of 37 degrees Fahrenheit (3 degrees Celsius). Temperatures average a balmy 78 degrees Fahrenheit (26 degrees Celsius) in July. During the nineteenth century, Washingtonians dreaded the hot, humid days of summer, which often brought epidemics of malaria and yellow fever from the mosquito-infested marshes.

Washington receives an average of 50 inches (127 centimeters) of precipitation over the course of the year. Summers tend to be rainy, and sleet and snow often snarl winter traffic. In January 1922, a blizzard buried the city under a record 25 inches (64 centimeters) of snow.

Though summer and winter have their drawbacks, few can find fault with spring and fall in Washington. In spring, the city comes alive with flowers and birdsong. In the fall, the changing foliage paints the brisk, breezy days with orange and crimson.

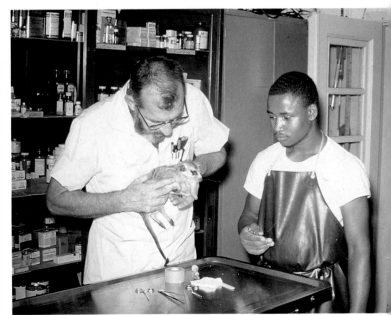

Chapter 3
THE CITY AND ITS PEOPLE

THE CITY AND ITS PEOPLE

Washington is a beautiful place . . . made beautiful by its trees, skies, fogs, rivers, and low green hills, and by the rich chaos of its buildings, a chaos subdued by its magnificently ordered plan.
—Elbert Peets, Federal Writers' Project, 1942

THE GRAND DESIGN

Unlike many American cities that grew haphazardly around a harbor or industrial center, Washington developed according to an orderly plan. It was originally designed to be the nation's capital, and it has served that purpose ever since.

Washington is laid out in a grid pattern. Its east-west streets are designated by letters of the alphabet, while its north-south streets are numbered. Broad diagonal avenues, named for states of the Union, crisscross the city.

Washington is enhanced by numerous squares and circles, islands of greenery amid the city's stone and concrete facades. The Mall, a broad sweep of lawns and trees, extends from the Washington Monument to the Capitol.

The District of Columbia (often referred to as "the District" or simply "D.C.") is divided into four geographic sections that radiate from the Capitol. The Mall and East Capitol Street break the city into north and south, and North Capitol and South Capitol streets serve as the boundary between east and west. Thus, a house that is south of the Mall and west of South Capitol Street is in Southwest Washington, and an office building north of East

Capitol and east of North Capitol is in the Northeast section. In terms of both area and population, Northwest Washington is the city's largest section.

WHO ARE THE WASHINGTONIANS?

Washington, D.C., has a population of 638,432, according to the 1980 census. In terms of population, it ranks ninth among American cities. Washington is the hub of a sprawling metropolitan area that spills into Montgomery, Prince Georges, Calvert, Charles, and Frederick counties in Maryland; Arlington, Fairfax, Loudoun, Prince William, and Stafford counties in Virginia; and the Virginia cities of Alexandria, Fairfax, Falls Church, Manassas, and Manassas Park, which are not part of any county. Of the approximately 3,250,822 people who live in metropolitan Washington, about 374,000 are government employees.

Black people have played a major role in Washington since its earliest history. In 1960, Washington became the first major American city to claim a black majority in population. Today,

19

**People of every ethnic background and
national origin live in Washington.**

about 70 percent of all Washingtonians are black. In contrast, the
capital's suburbs in Maryland and Virginia are about 78 percent
white.

People of every ethnic background and national origin live in
Washington. Many of Washington's foreign-born residents work
for embassies or for international organizations with headquarters
in the city. Hispanic families, comprising almost 3 percent of the
city's population, are concentrated in the Adams-Morgan section
of Northwest Washington. Asians are a small but rapidly growing
minority group. White Washingtonians, comprising about 27
percent of the capital's population, live in neighborhoods
throughout the city, but primarily in the Northwest.

Washington is a city of contradictions. With an average annual
income of $12,039 in 1980, Washington had higher per capita
earnings than any state except Alaska. Yet many Washingtonians
suffer devastating poverty, living in neighborhoods plagued by
low employment and high crime rates. About 14 percent of the
people in Washington receive some form of public assistance.

The Washington metropolitan area includes neighborhoods such as
Georgetown (above) as well as nearby counties in Maryland and Virginia.

POLITICS

Politics is another realm in which Washington is beset with
contradictions. The capital of the world's largest democracy,
Washington had no representative government between 1874 and
1974. Washington citizens were not permitted to vote in
presidential elections until 1964, and do not have voting
representatives in Congress.

Since they won the right to vote for president, Washingtonians
have proved to be overwhelmingly Democratic. In the 1972
landslide victory of Republican Richard Nixon, only
Massachusetts and the District of Columbia cast their electoral
votes for Democratic candidate George McGovern. In 1984, when
the nation reelected Republican Ronald Reagan, his Democratic
opponent Walter Mondale carried only the District and his home
state of Minnesota.

Chapter 4

THE FOUNDING OF THE CAPITAL

THE FOUNDING OF THE CAPITAL

*Although the means now within the power of the country
are not such as to pursue the design to any great extent . . .
the plan should be drawn on such a scale as to leave room
for the aggrandizement and the embellishment which an
increase in the wealth of the nation will permit it
to pursue at any period, however remote.*
— Pierre-Charles L'Enfant, 1791

When he wrote to George Washington in the letter from which
the quote above was taken, L'Enfant knew that his plans and
hopes for a magnificent capital city would not be realized in his
lifetime. Generations passed before L'Enfant's ambitious design
could be transformed into reality.

THE FIRST WASHINGTONIANS

Just east of Rock Creek Park in Northwest Washington, D.C.,
archaeologists have uncovered the remains of an ancient
soapstone quarry. For hundreds of years before Europeans
reached the Potomac, Native American people excavated stone
that was used to make arrowheads, hatchet blades, scrapers, and
other tools.

When Europeans arrived early in the 1600s, a group of people
called the Piscataways lived at the site of present-day Washington.
They belonged to the large Algonquian family of tribes, whose

The Native American people who lived in the Washington region used a number of different methods to catch fish.

members shared similar languages and customs. The Piscataways lived in villages surrounded by stake fences, or palisades. They raised corn, squash, and other vegetables, and used woven nets to catch fish in the Potomac and the Anacostia.

Never a powerful people, the Piscataways were dominated by the warlike Iroquois who lived to the north. When English colonies arose in Virginia and Maryland, the Piscataways tried to form an alliance with their new neighbors. But smallpox and other European diseases, for which the Indians had no immunity, devastated the tribe. In 1680, the surviving Piscataways abandoned their villages in the Washington region and moved farther up the Potomac. They were eventually absorbed by the league of Iroquois nations.

The first European to live on the site of Washington was probably an English fur trapper named Henry Fleete, who arrived in 1632. Two years later, the land that is now the District of Columbia became part of England's Maryland colony, under Governor Leonard Calvert.

In its early years, much of Maryland was divided into large tobacco-growing estates, or manors. The biggest and most valuable estate within present-day Washington was Duddington Manor, founded in 1663. The lords of the manors enjoyed horse races, fencing matches, and an endless round of parties at which the finest foods and wines were served. Much of the actual work on the manor was done by slaves imported from Africa.

The Marylanders were eager to trade with the other British colonies and with Europe. In 1751, they founded a trading port called Georgetown on the Potomac River west of Rock Creek. Georgetown and Alexandria, on the other side of the Potomac in Virginia, soon flourished. The colonists hoped these towns would some day compete with Philadelphia and New York.

In 1776, the thirteen British colonies along the Atlantic Coast declared themselves independent from the mother country, after launching the long and bloody Revolutionary War in 1775. The Treaty of Paris, signed in 1783, created a new but uncertain nation in North America. The former colonies were faced with many challenges. What sort of government would enable them to function together harmoniously? And where should they establish their capital city?

THE SITE ON THE POTOMAC

The American capital shifted restlessly—from Philadelphia to Princeton, New Jersey, to New York. A permanent capital was desperately needed, but debate raged over its location. Delegates from the southern states hoped to establish a capital city in the

South, while northerners pressed for a site in New Jersey, New York, or Pennsylvania.

The nation's first president, George Washington, favored building the capital somewhere on the lower reaches of the Potomac River. Washington wanted the capital to be a great port and a gateway to the western frontier. He believed that the Potomac would be a key route to the Atlantic Ocean and to the developing lands west of the Allegheny Mountains.

In 1790, the delegates at last agreed that the capital should be located on the Potomac. George Washington selected a site across the river from Mount Vernon, his home in Virginia. Lying almost at the midpoint between the southern and northern states, the location was a compromise that all could accept.

The state of Maryland donated about 70 square miles (181 square kilometers) of land, including the port of Georgetown, to the newly created Federal District. In addition, approximately 30 square miles (78 square kilometers) of the original district were contributed by Virginia. (The portion of the capital south of the Potomac, which included the port of Alexandria, was returned to Virginia in 1846.)

Congress moved temporarily to Philadelphia, but ordered that the new capital be ready by 1800. To design a city that would meet the government's practical needs yet be a symbol of the nation's great potential, President Washington chose a brilliant young French engineer named Pierre-Charles L'Enfant.

L'Enfant was an art student in Paris when he volunteered to serve with the Continental army during the American Revolution. After the war, he helped plan renovations of Federal Hall, where Congress met for a time in New York. He also designed the Purple Heart, which is awarded to wounded American soldiers.

After receiving his appointment from the president, L'Enfant

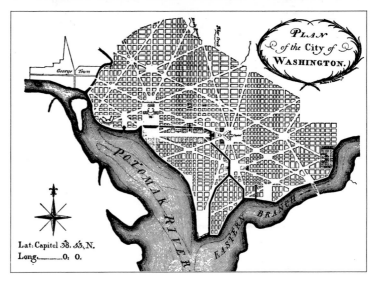

The plan for Washington (above) created by Pierre-Charles L'Enfant (left) made the Capitol the center of the city.

spent three weeks exploring the site on horseback and on foot. He saw glorious possibilities in the woods and marshes along the Potomac. He envisioned a city of sweeping vistas and splendid monuments, a city to rival the most magnificent capitals in Europe. He pictured the Presidential Palace, a noble statue of George Washington, and, on Jenkins Hill at the very center of the city, the Federal House, or Capitol.

To many people in the struggling new nation, L'Enfant's ideas seemed impractical, even ridiculous. Farmers in the Federal District complained that his grand avenues, some of them more than 160 feet (49 meters) wide, wasted valuable cropland. Not one for making compromises, L'Enfant quarreled endlessly with the commissioners who had been appointed to work with him.

At first, President Washington tried to soothe the commissioners, hoping that L'Enfant's plan could be carried out peaceably. But when L'Enfant made an enemy of Commissioner Daniel Carroll, heir to Duddington Manor, the president was forced to take action. Carroll had begun to construct a new manor house, but it stood in the path of one of L'Enfant's avenues. When

Benjamin Banneker and Andrew Ellicott carried out L'Enfant's plans with only minor modifications.

Carroll refused to build somewhere else, L'Enfant ordered his work crew to tear the house down.

In January 1792, George Washington dismissed L'Enfant, and Congress offered him $2,500 for his efforts. L'Enfant refused this sum, which he felt was far too small. He never received a penny for his work, and died in poverty in 1825.

In L'Enfant's place, President Washington appointed Andrew Ellicott, who had already been working on the project as a surveyor. Ellicott's assistant was Benjamin Banneker, a self-educated free black man who was a prominent astronomer and mathematician. With minor modifications, Ellicott and Banneker continued to carry out L'Enfant's plans.

To L'Enfant, Jenkins Hill was a ''pedestal waiting for a monument.'' While serving as city planner, he chose the spot as the ideal location for the Congress House, or Capitol. A prize of $500 was offered to the person who created the best design for the Capitol. The contest deadline came and passed, and the judges were disappointed with all of the entries. One would-be designer wanted to crown the Capitol with a giant weathercock.

At last, several months after the contest had officially closed, the judges received an entry from Dr. William Thornton. Thornton was a man of many talents—a physician, a portrait painter, an inventor, and an amateur architect. He designed a Capitol with two wings joined by a domed central hall. The committee of judges unanimously approved his plan. George Washington, too, was delighted, and praised the plan for its "grandeur, simplicity, and convenience." In a gala ceremony on September 25, 1793, George Washington laid the cornerstone for the new United States Capitol.

Progress was slow over the following years. But in 1800, according to schedule, the federal government moved to take up residence in the half-finished city.

WASHINGTON, NATIONAL CAPITAL

In June 1800, a small cavalcade of wagons rumbled into the Federal District, bearing the worldly possessions of the 126 men and women who were the nation's government workers. The country's official papers were shipped from Philadelphia by water. On November 2, John Adams became the first president to move into the Presidential Palace. On his first night in his new home, Adams wrote to his wife Abigail: "I pray heaven to bestow the best of blessings on this house, and all that shall hereafter inhabit it. May none but honest and wise men ever rule under this roof."

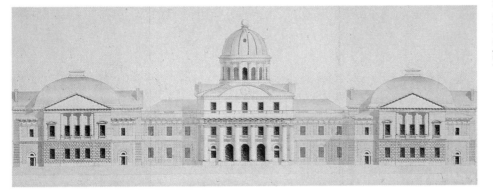

Entries in the Capitol design competition included a building topped by a huge weathervane (top), the second-place design by Stephen Hallet (middle), and the winning design by Dr. William Thornton (bottom).

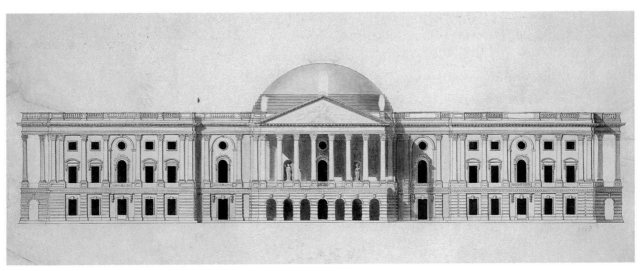

President George Washington laid the cornerstone for the Capitol in 1793.

When Abigail Adams arrived a few weeks later, she found the Presidential Palace still under construction, surrounded by brickyards and rubble. "We have not the least fence, yard, or other convenience without," she wrote in a letter to her daughter, "and the great unfinished audience room [the present East Room] I make a drying-room of, to hang the clothes in." Nevertheless, she remained optimistic, and concluded: "[Washington] is a beautiful spot, capable of every improvement; and the more I view it, the more I am delighted with it."

Few would argue that improvements were badly needed. Of the three hundred streets that L'Enfant had planned, only three had been completed. Cows grazed along the roadsides, and cornfields straggled among the scattered houses. One visiting New Yorker quipped, "We only need more houses, cellars, kitchens, scholarly men, amiable women, and a few other such trifles to possess a perfect city."

Like the Presidential Palace, the Federal House was only partially completed in 1800. On November 22, Congress held its first session in the North Wing while workmen were still busy in other parts of the building. President Adams addressed a joint congressional session on this momentous occasion: "I congratulate the people of the United States on the assembling of Congress at the permanent seat of their government. . . . In this city may that piety and virtue, that wisdom and magnanimity, that constancy and self-government which adorned the great character whose name it bears be forever held in veneration."

WASHINGTON IN FLAMES

By the close of its first decade as the nation's capital, Washington was still a half-built city with a "wild, desolate air from being so scantily and rudely cultivated," in the words of one British minister. Gradually, however, high society began to take root in the town on the Potomac. Dolley Madison, the charming wife of President James Madison, became famous for organizing elegant parties at the Presidential Palace. But new trials loomed just ahead.

For several years, the United States had vied with Great Britain for control of the high seas. In 1812, the hostilities flared into war. The young American nation was ill-prepared to fight the mighty British navy, and British ships attacked many ports on the Atlantic Coast.

On August 24, 1814, a poorly trained band of militiamen tried in vain to fend off a British assault on Bladensburg, Maryland, just outside the District of Columbia. The Americans were soundly defeated in a battle that some nicknamed the "Bladensburg Races." With the militia out of the way, British forces under Admiral George Cockburn and General Robert Ross marched boldly into the unguarded capital. Fearing the worst, government

In 1814, during the War of 1812, the British marched into Washington and burned many government buildings, including the White House.

workers loaded valuable documents onto wagons and carried them to safety outside the city. Dolley Madison rescued a priceless portrait of George Washington, painted by prominent American artist Gilbert Stuart, just before the British set fire to the Presidential Palace.

Throughout that evening and much of the following day, the British set Washington's public buildings ablaze. In addition to the Presidential Palace, they burned the arsenal, the Capitol, and the offices of the Cabinet members. Some witnesses claimed that Cockburn burst into the House chambers, sat in the speaker's chair, and asked mockingly, "Shall this harbor of Yankee democracy be burned?" "Aye!" his men roared, and put the torch to the House and Senate wings.

Some British officers, however, seemed to have qualms about what they were doing. As the British prepared to set the federal patent office afire, William Thornton protested that the records of inventions that were stored there belonged not only to the American government, but to the world. After his eloquent speech, the Patent Office Building was spared.

An eloquent speech by William Thornton persuaded the British not to set fire to the Patent Office Building.

The Capitol and many other buildings were saved from total destruction by a violent thunderstorm that swept the city on the afternoon of August 25. Torrential rain put out many of the fires. To further discourage the invaders, an ammunition explosion killed several British soldiers. At the same time, rumors flew through the British ranks that American reinforcements were on the way. Hastily, the British withdrew. Behind them, the buildings that had symbolized the hopes and ideals of the young nation still smoldered, and the air hung cloudy with ashes.

The attack demoralized many Washingtonians, and some even talked of abandoning the city forever. "I do not suppose the government will ever return to Washington," wrote one society woman. "All those whose property is invested in that place will be reduced to poverty."

For several weeks, Congress debated making a move. But news of a stunning American victory in the Battle of New Orleans helped to renew the nation's confidence. Congress voted to stay in Washington. Workmen cleared the charred rubble and began the task of building the capital once more.

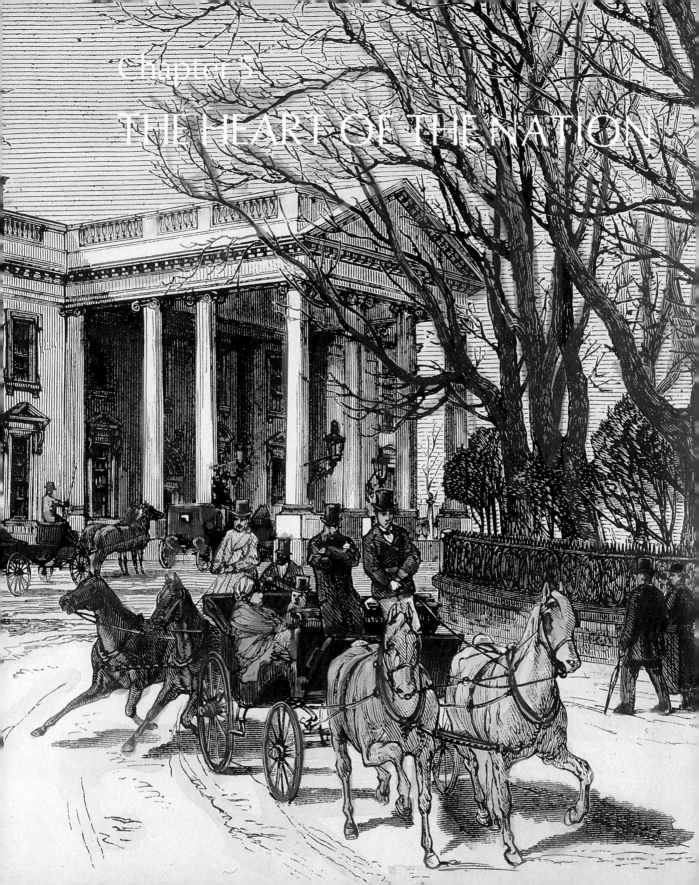

Chapter 5
THE HEART OF THE NATION

THE HEART OF THE NATION

Washington society is singularly compounded from the
largest variety of elements: foreign ambassadors,
members of Congress . . . flippant young belles and pious
wives dutifully attending their husbands . . . grave judges,
saucy travelers, pert newspaper reporters, melancholy
Indian chiefs and timid New England ladies. . . . All this
is wholly unlike anything that is to be seen in
any other city in the world.
—Harriet Martineau, 1835

When writer Harriet Martineau painted the portrait of
Washington quoted above, the United States was feeling its
growing power and strength. As the capital of this thriving young
nation, Washington hummed with excitement. But soon the
nation's very existence would be in danger, and once again
Washington would be a city at war.

FROM TOWN TO CITY

George Washington had wanted the capital city to be a center of
industry and trade. But by the 1820s, Washington was still a small
town in many ways. Dozens of its streets remained unpaved and
full of stumps and potholes. Oil lamps had been installed around
the Presidential Palace, but the city could not afford to buy fuel to
light them. The lamps served simply as ornaments. The
president's house stood unlocked and unguarded. During the

An 1832 view of Washington

administration of Martin Van Buren, a man wandered in off the street and fell asleep on a drawing-room sofa.

With its waterfalls and snakelike curves, the Potomac proved impractical as a trade route to the western frontier. The Chesapeake and Ohio Canal, begun at Georgetown in 1828, eventually linked the District with the lands beyond the Alleghenies. But by that time, Baltimore had far outstripped Washington as a center of commerce. In industry, too, Washington lagged dismally behind Baltimore and such northern cities as New York and Philadelphia. Washington had only one real business—the United States government.

When Congress was in session, Washington bustled with activity. Congressmen and foreign diplomats brought an air of sophistication to the town on the Potomac. Elegant carriages clattered down the half-finished streets, and lavishly dressed men and women called at the finest houses. People from all over the growing nation flocked to Washington, hoping to gain the ear of the government.

Yet life could be cruel for Washington's black residents. Thousands of free blacks worked as barbers, shoemakers, and plasterers, and in dozens of other trades. A few even became wealthy. One black merchant, Alfred Lee, bought a mansion on H Street that had formerly served as the British Embassy. But thousands of other black men, women, and children were slaves, owned by the well-to-do families of the city.

Slavery had been an institution in Washington since its founding. The city was also a center for trading in slaves. Conditions in the slave pens, where the human merchandise was kept awaiting sale, were appalling. John Randolph, himself a slaveholder, protested, "You call this the land of liberty, and every day things are done in it at which the despotisms of Europe would be horror-struck and disgusted. . . . In no part of the earth . . . is there so great, so infamous a slave market, as in the metropolis, in the seat of government of this nation which prides itself on freedom."

Despite the contradictions in Washington's existence, work on its public buildings marched resolutely on. President Andrew Jackson ordered the completion of the East Room of the Presidential Palace, where Abigail Adams had once hung her laundry, and transformed it into a magnificent ballroom. After the 1814 fire, the president's home was painted white, and Jackson began to call it the White House.

Jackson also began work on the United States Treasury Building. He had a stormy relationship with Congress, and according to legend, he ordered the Treasury Building to be constructed beside the White House where it would block his view of Capitol Hill.

The death of an Englishman named James Smithson, who had never set foot in the United States, was to have a profound effect on the intellectual life of Washington. Disenchanted with European aristocracy, Smithson came to admire America's

The ornate structure known as the Castle was the Smithsonian's first building.

democratic ideals. When he died in 1829, he willed his vast fortune to the United States. According to the will, the money was to be used "to found in Washington, under the name Smithsonian Institution, an establishment for the increase and diffusion of knowledge among men."

Nine years after Smithson's death, 105 bags of gold coins, worth half a million dollars, arrived in Washington. In this modern age of multibillion-dollar budgets, the sum does not sound very remarkable. But in 1838, it was one of the greatest fortunes in the world. Debate raged in Congress over how this extraordinary gift should be used. Former president John Quincy Adams suggested the founding of a museum, and in 1846 an act of Congress created the Smithsonian Institution.

The Smithsonian's first building, the ornate structure known as the Castle, opened on the Mall in 1852. Its early displays included botanical specimens from scientific expeditions to Asia and Africa, George Washington's surveying instruments, and gowns worn by the nation's First Ladies.

During the enlargement of the Capitol between 1851 and 1865, the original dome was removed (right) and a larger one was built.

In 1848, construction began on the monument to George Washington that L'Enfant had envisioned when he drew up his original plan. Two years later, workmen began to enlarge the Capitol to meet the needs of the expanding federal government. Little by little, it seemed, Washington was growing into its role as capital of one of the world's great nations.

A DIVIDED CITY

On July 4, 1851, Massachusetts Senator Daniel Webster spoke at the cornerstone ceremony for the new wing of the Capitol. "If it shall hereafter be the will of God that this structure shall fall from its base," Webster declared, "... be it then known that on this day the Union of the United States stands firm, that their Constitution still exists unimpaired and with all its original usefulness and glory."

The winged statue of Freedom, designed by sculptor Thomas Crawford, crowns the Capitol dome.

Webster's words reflected the tensions that had begun to threaten the American Union he loved. Since the 1830s, a movement for the abolition of slavery had gained power in the northern states. But slavery was part of the southern way of life and, many southerners believed, essential to the South's economy. In Congress, delegates argued passionately on both sides of the slavery question. The Compromise of 1850 limited the expansion of slavery into western states entering the Union, and prohibited the sale of slaves in Washington. But the underlying issue was still unresolved.

In Washington, the winged statue of Freedom that crowned the new Capitol dome became a focus of the bitter slavery debate. Originally, sculptor Thomas Crawford had depicted Freedom in a type of feathered headgear that was worn by liberated slaves in ancient Rome. Many southerners, led by Senator Jefferson Davis of Mississippi, protested that the statue carried an abolitionist message. To appease them, the feathers were finally changed to resemble an American Indian headdress.

As rumors spread that the slave states might secede from the Union, many white Washingtonians were sympathetic to their cause. Some 3,100 slaves and more than 11,000 free black people lived in Washington by 1860. Whites lived in fear of a slave uprising, led by the more mobile and better-educated free blacks. Strict laws forbade blacks from gathering without permits, and forced them to obey a 10:00 P.M. curfew.

To the horror of most southerners, the candidate of the antislavery Republican party, Abraham Lincoln, won the election of 1860. Almost at once, rumors of secession became fact. First South Carolina withdrew from the Union, followed by one southern state after another. If the slaveholding states of Virginia and Maryland seceded, the federal capital would be an island, entirely surrounded by hostile territory.

On Inauguration Day, Lincoln swept down Pennsylvania Avenue, closely flanked by federal troops. Marksmen with rifles watched from housetops for any signs of trouble. The windows of the Capitol bristled with guns, and ranks of soldiers kept back the crowd as Lincoln mounted the inaugural platform. "I hold that . . . the union of these states is perpetual," Lincoln told the throngs of spectators. "No state, upon its own mere notion, can lawfully get out of the Union. The power confided to me will be used to hold, occupy, and possess the property and places belonging to the government."

On April 12, 1861, Lincoln's promise was put to the first test when Confederate cannons fired on Union-held Fort Sumter in Charleston, South Carolina. Three days later, Lincoln sent out a call for volunteers to swell the ranks of the Union army. The divided nation plunged into civil war.

President Abraham Lincoln gave his first inaugural address on March 4, 1861, only a month or so before the outbreak of the Civil War.

WASHINGTON AT WAR

Days after the attack on Fort Sumter, Virginia left the Union to join the newly formed Confederate States of America. The slogan "On to Washington" rang throughout the South. From the White House, Lincoln could see the Confederate flag floating above Alexandria across the Potomac. Prosouthern mobs in nearby Baltimore tore up railroad tracks and severed telegraph wires, cutting off Washington's communication with the North. If Washington were attacked, many feared, Confederate sympathizers within the city might hand the capital over to the enemy.

Author Louisa May Alcott (left), nurse Clara Barton (right), and poet Walt Whitman were among those who worked tirelessly in the Washington hospital wards during the Civil War.

For four days, Washington waited in terror for the siege to begin. At last, the Seventh Regiment from New York marched into the city, and the panic subsided. "An indescribable gloom had hung over Washington for nearly a week, paralyzing its traffic and crushing out its life," wrote eyewitness John Hay. "The presence of this single regiment seemed to turn the scales of fate."

Washington had survived the first crisis, but four grueling years of war still lay ahead. In July 1861, an eager band of Union troops set out from Washington to assail the Confederate forces along a Virginia creek called Bull Run. Thrilled at the chance to see a real battle, one that surely would end the war once and for all, women in carriages followed the marching soldiers. But the Confederates were armed and ready, and quickly routed the Yankee invaders. As they hastened back to Washington, the retreating troops found the roads clogged with startled picnickers.

During the war, Washington became the major supply depot and hospital camp for the biggest army the Western Hemisphere had ever seen. The city's population exploded from seventy-five thousand in 1860 to one hundred thousand by the war's end in 1865. There were regiments of soldiers to guard the capital against invasion; hordes of wounded men needing treatment; and streams of black refugees from the Confederacy, many of them eager to enlist in the Union army. The swelling population strained Washington's resources beyond their limits. Food and water supplies ran low. Tiber Creek became a stinking open sewer, and epidemics of typhoid and dysentery swept the city.

Hundreds of private homes and even parts of the Capitol, still under construction, served as military barracks. Brick ovens were set up in committee rooms in the Capitol basement, and army bakers fed troops throughout the city.

Churches, homes, and warehouses were turned into hospitals, and volunteers did their best to care for the wounded and sick. Among the most dedicated nurses was a quiet young woman named Clara Barton, who had previously been a clerk in the patent office. Years later, her Civil War experiences inspired her to found the American Red Cross. Louisa May Alcott, best known as the author of *Little Women,* and poet Walt Whitman also worked tirelessly in the makeshift hospital wards. "The hurt and wounded I pacify with soothing hand," wrote Whitman in 1862. "I sit by the restless all the dark night. Some are so young!"

Appointed by Lincoln to handle the capital's defense, General George B. McClellan amassed a force of two hundred thousand men in the Army of the Potomac. The city streets became parade grounds as he mercilessly drilled his troops, earning the nickname "McNapoleon."

In July 1864, Confederate forces under General Jubal Early crossed the Upper Potomac and marched through Maryland to Silver Spring, just north of Washington. Frightened and fascinated, thousands of Washingtonians rushed into the streets. Even the president left the White House to watch the battle from the parapet of Fort Stevens on Thirteenth Street. When a man standing beside Lincoln was killed, a young army officer named Oliver Wendell Holmes (later to become chief justice of the Supreme Court) shouted at the president, "Get down, you fool!" Reluctantly, Lincoln crouched down. When he rose and brushed himself off, he commented, "Young man, I'm glad you know how to speak to a civilian."

Marching into Washington from the south, General Ulysses S. Grant brought reinforcements that drove Early back from the city. Over the following months, the rebels lost more and more ground. After Grant captured the Confederate capital at Richmond, Virginia, the South finally surrendered.

The war years left Lincoln gaunt and exhausted. Yet when his wife arranged for him to attend a play less than a week after the treaty of peace had been signed, he felt he ought to go, to make a public appearance. On the night of April 14, 1865, Lincoln and his wife sat in their box at Ford's Theatre. Unnoticed by the audience, an actor named John Wilkes Booth crept into the presidential box. Suddenly raising a gun, Booth shot Lincoln in the back of the head. Lincoln slumped forward as Booth sprang from the box shouting, *Sic semper tyrannis!* (Virginia's state motto, "Thus Always to Tyrants"), and fled from the theater.

As the crowd stared in shock and disbelief, Lincoln was carried to a house across the street, where he died early the following morning. Telegraph wires sped the tragic news across the nation. Thousands of mourners flocked to the Capitol Rotunda, where Lincoln's body lay in state. The president's coffin was then loaded onto a black-draped train for the long journey to its final resting place in Springfield, Illinois. At every stop along the way, grieving

President Lincoln's funeral train is shown here at the Baltimore & Ohio station just before its long journey to Springfield, Illinois.

crowds paid homage to the man who had sacrificed so much to save the Union.

WASHINGTON IN THE GILDED AGE

The pressures of its mushrooming population left Washington in deplorable condition after the war. The roads turned to mud at every rain, clean drinking water was in short supply, and the sanitation system was a menace to public health. Poor people, most of them newly freed slaves, lived in shacks in a maze of alleys behind the city's comfortable houses.

Most former slaves, or freedmen, had done agricultural work all their lives. They had few skills that could be put to use in Washington, where government was virtually the only industry. Many freedmen found work as domestic servants, or became barbers, grocers, or skilled tradesmen. Thousands more, however,

Howard University was established by the Freedmen's Bureau in 1867.

could not find work of any kind. Some picked through garbage dumps in search of scraps of food, and others resorted to petty crime in their fight for survival.

In 1865, Congress created the Freedmen's Bureau to foster the education and employment of former slaves. The Freedmen's Bureau, as well as many black community groups, founded schools for black children throughout the city. In 1867, the bureau established Howard University, which grew to become the foremost black university in the nation. In that same year, blacks won two seats on Washington's twenty-member governing council.

The most prominent member of the city council in the late 1860s was an ambitious local builder named Alexander Shepherd. Born into poverty, Shepherd worked as a plumber and eventually made a fortune in real estate. In 1870, he was appointed to Washington's Board of Public Works. Within months, he announced a bold plan to renovate the city.

Over the next three years, Shepherd's crews paved 80 miles (129 kilometers) of streets, planted trees, and dug sewers. They covered over the fetid Tiber Creek and transformed it into Constitution Avenue. Typhoid and dysentery declined, and foreign governments invested money in the city.

But Shepherd's project cost far more than Congress had allotted. By 1874, Washington was $18 million in debt. After a thorough investigation into Shepherd's operations, the Senate relieved him of his office, and his improvement programs ground to a halt.

Since 1820, Washingtonians had elected a mayor and a city council, although the federal government provided most of the city's revenue. Shepherd's financial crisis persuaded Congress that Washington could not govern itself responsibly. In 1874, Congress placed the city under the control of three commissioners to be appointed by the president. The people of Washington lost the right to vote for public officials. The capital of the world's largest democracy was being governed like a colonial territory.

Some historians believe that Congress ended home rule in Washington because whites feared black political power. With the city's large black population, black people could have had considerable control over the city's affairs. Some whites preferred to end voting altogether rather than let blacks go to the polls. Other historians argue that major bank failures in 1873 and scandals during the Republican administration of President Ulysses S. Grant prompted the Democratic Congress to resume control of District government.

Washington's high society flourished in the last decades of the nineteenth century. As one observer commented, there were "diamonds in every hotel parlor, capitalists in the Senate, [and] state dinners unsurpassed among officials." In the 1890s, fashionable hostesses organized parties around a color theme, where everything from the decorations and the guests' costumes to the ice cream had to be of a particular color. There were balls, concerts, and evenings at the theater. While the city's poor people struggled, the wealthy and privileged enjoyed an era remembered as Washington's Gilded Age.

Chapter 6
WASHINGTON AND THE WORLD

WASHINGTON AND THE WORLD

The ultimate power lies in Washington. . . .
It is in Washington that the great domestic
crises must be dealt with, and the great crises
of foreign policy, too, up to and including
the ultimate choice between peace and war.
—Stuart Alsop, a Washington journalist

A WAR TO END ALL WARS

Under Washington's new commissioner form of government, Congress controlled the city's budget. By the beginning of the twentieth century, Congress's support for city services such as schools and street repairs had dwindled to a trickle. But the budget had room for extravagant schemes to beautify the city. In 1902, workmen cleared away the decaying railway yards and warehouses along the Mall, and turned it into the elegant parkway L'Enfant had intended. Gleaming new congressional office buildings sprang up on either side of the Capitol. To the north rose the magnificent Union Station.

On April 6, 1917, the United States entered the vast, bloody war that had gripped Europe for the previous three years. Washington flung itself into the war effort. Flags flew over shops and houses, and soldiers paraded through the streets. Thousands of men and women poured into the city to take jobs in newly created government "war bureaus." Temporary office buildings popped up like mushrooms along the Mall, and the grand plaza in front of

Warren G. Harding (second from left) was the first president to ride in an automobile instead of a horse-drawn carriage in the inaugural parade.

Union Station was crowded with dormitories for government workers.

During the nineteen months the United States was engaged in the "Great War," statesmen and military experts from the Allied nations hastened to Washington to consult with President Woodrow Wilson and other high officials. The center of American expertise and power, Washington stood at the fulcrum of the Allied war effort.

BIG CITY, BIG GOVERNMENT

The 1920s brought major changes to Washington. Cars transformed the face of the city, bringing outlying suburbs closer but creating enormous traffic jams on streets and bridges. In 1921, Warren G. Harding became the first president to ride in an automobile instead of a horse-drawn carriage in the inaugural parade down Pennsylvania Avenue.

Year by year, the federal government expanded, outgrowing its original offices and demanding more and more space. Under

President Calvin Coolidge, work began on a new complex of buildings between Pennsylvania and Constitution avenues and east of Fifteenth Street. This "Federal Triangle" included new headquarters for the Post Office, the National Archives, and the Departments of Labor, Commerce, and Justice.

In 1922, crowds gathered for the dedication of the Lincoln Memorial. The seated statue of Lincoln, head bowed in thought, became a symbol of the struggle for freedom in America. Ironically, four years later, the United States Supreme Court upheld a new law that forbade people who were black or Jewish to move into many District neighborhoods. Other housing codes began to exclude Arabs, Eastern Europeans, and, as one newspaper columnist put it, "everybody except me and thee, with some doubts about thee."

The 1920s brought prosperity to most parts of the United States. But in 1929, the stock market crashed in New York, heralding the most devastating economic depression the nation had ever known. Some 15 million Americans lost their jobs. In Washington, one worker out of every four became unemployed.

Veterans of the World War were due to receive a substantial bonus for their services by 1945. In the early years of the depression, they began asking Congress to issue the bonus money immediately, to help them in their desperate need. In 1932, an army of "bonus marchers" arrived in Washington—some riding in boxcars, some in rusted old jalopies, and many on foot— to petition Congress in person.

Thousands of bonus marchers settled in a hastily erected shantytown on the Anacostia Flats. Living by the slogan "No radical talk, no panhandling, no booze," they demonstrated peacefully on the Capitol grounds. After the Senate voted down the proposed Bonus Bill, most of the ragged men and their families set out for home. But about ten thousand disgruntled marchers remained in Washington. Fearing trouble, President Herbert Hoover ordered the United States Army to evict them. Federal troops paraded down Pennsylvania Avenue, crossed the Anacostia, and set fire to the shantytown.

Throughout their stay in Washington, the bonus marchers had been peaceful and law-abiding. Yet, to justify the government's action, the attorney general claimed that "the marchers brought the largest aggregation of criminals that was ever assembled in the city at one time."

In a cold drizzling rain on March 4, 1933, Franklin D. Roosevelt was sworn in as the nation's thirty-second president. From a platform over the Capitol steps, Roosevelt told the troubled nation, "The only thing we have to fear is fear itself." His words had scarcely been uttered when the rain stopped and the sun broke through the clouds.

Hoover had tried to control the Great Depression by cutting government spending. Roosevelt's New Deal, on the other hand, used the government to create jobs, putting millions of people back to work across the country. By 1934, about forty thousand people a day poured through Washington's Union Station, eager to look for federal jobs in the capital.

The government's rapidly expanding programs hired thousands of these newcomers as minor officials, clerks, messengers, and construction workers. Yet there was still not enough work for the endless stream of job seekers. Many of them were black farm workers from the South who had little education and few marketable skills. A District law denied relief payments to any family with "an employable father." Under this rule, many men were forced to leave home so that their wives and children could receive public assistance.

In 1932, thousands of unemployed World War I veterans, protesting the Senate's decision not to give them a bonus, were evicted from their Washington shantytown by federal troops.

One social worker protested to the chairman of the House District Committee, which regulated the city's budget. She argued that the law destroyed families, and asked that assistance be granted to all needy people without restrictions. "If I went along with your ideas, I would never keep my seat in Congress," replied the chairman, a representative from Mississippi. "My constituents would not stand for spending all that money on Negroes."

During the New Deal era, many fine new buildings and monuments rose in Washington. The Supreme Court, with its dazzling pink-and-white marble facade, was completed in 1935. In 1937, work began on the National Gallery of Art on the Mall. The Jefferson Memorial was planned for a spot on the edge of the Tidal Basin. As construction on the monument got underway, protesters chained themselves to the Japanese cherry trees that had beautified the Tidal Basin since 1912. The monument was finally built, leaving most of the trees unharmed.

A crowd gathered at the White House gates shortly after President Roosevelt announced that the Japanese had attacked the American fleet at Pearl Harbor.

On the afternoon of December 7, 1941, the nation was shocked by the news that Japanese planes had attacked the American naval fleet at Pearl Harbor. That night, hundreds of people gathered in Lafayette Square. In awestruck silence, they gazed at the White House across the street. It blazed with lights. Behind its closed doors, diplomats, Cabinet members, and generals met with the president to chart the course of the Second World War.

During the war, Washington was again flooded with newcomers eager for work, this time in government war offices. The capital was the hub of the vast Allied war effort, where officials from twenty-six nations met to discuss strategies and concerns. In the fall of 1944, American, British, Russian, and Chinese delegates met at Dumbarton Oaks, a mansion in Northwest Washington, to plan an organization of nations that could work to prevent future wars. When the war was finally over, the United States helped to create the United Nations.

THE ERA OF CHANGE

In the years after World War II, Washington's population continued to grow. More and more government workers chose to live in nearby suburbs and commute to their jobs in the city. Many federal bureaus and departments set up headquarters in Maryland and Virginia. Throughout Washington's sprawling metropolitan area rang the demand for more housing, more office space, more highways.

The migration of black people from the rural South, which had begun during the depression, continued throughout the 1950s. By 1960, blacks comprised 54 percent of Washington's population. Franklin Roosevelt had issued a code of rules meant to end the federal government's discriminatory hiring practices. Although this Fair Employment Practices Code was not always enforced, blacks had a better chance of finding work with the government than with most for-profit corporations. Even in civil service, however, black people were often channeled into menial positions with little opportunity for advancement.

During the 1950s and 1960s, Dr. Martin Luther King, Jr., an eloquent Baptist minister from Alabama, fought tirelessly to gain full civil rights for black people throughout the nation. On August 28, 1963, King led more than two hundred thousand marchers from the Washington Monument to the Lincoln Memorial in the largest civil-rights demonstration the nation had ever witnessed. At the Lincoln Memorial, King told the cheering crowd, "I have a dream that one day this nation will rise up and live out the true meaning of its creed, 'We hold these truths to be self-evident: that all men are created equal. . . . ' "

Only three months after King's historic march, the world was stunned by the news that President John F. Kennedy had been

In August 1963, Dr. Martin Luther King, Jr., spoke to a huge crowd of people who were demonstrating for full civil rights for all black people, many of whom held the most menial jobs in the country and lived in the poorest neighborhoods of the nation's cities.

shot and killed. In a great bronze coffin, Kennedy's body was carried from the East Room of the White House up Pennsylvania Avenue to the Capitol. The fallen president lay in state in the Capitol Rotunda, where Abraham Lincoln had lain nearly a century before. Later, dignitaries from all over the world followed the casket to St. Matthew's Cathedral, where the funeral service was delivered. Kennedy was laid to rest in Arlington National Cemetery, just across the Potomac from the capital.

THE ROAD TO HOME RULE

In 1965, President Lyndon B. Johnson introduced a bill into Congress that would allow the District of Columbia to govern itself. The bill triggered three days of debate so passionate that security guards cleared the visitors' gallery for fear of violence. When the time came for the final vote, however, Johnson's bill went down in defeat.

Since 1948, six similar home-rule bills had been proposed by United States presidents and passed by the Senate, only to bog down in the House Committee on the District of Columbia. Washington remained under the control of Congress and an appointed team of commissioners. Most of the capital's long-term residents felt that Congress was indifferent to their needs. Public schools were poorly staffed and ill-equipped, city hospitals were underfunded, and the people of Washington had no means to bring about change. As one journalist wrote, "Today's speeches about the glories of democracy should always be followed by the words, 'except in Washington.' The fact that those who live in the seat of democracy do not enjoy its basic prerogatives is quite literally incredible."

The frustrations of black Washingtonians boiled over on the evening of April 4, 1968, when word flashed across the nation that Martin Luther King, Jr., had been assassinated in Memphis, Tennessee. For three days, violence wracked Washington. Rioters looted stores and set fire to buildings. Nine people were killed, and 3,263 men and women were taken into custody. Finally, 11,000 federal troops occupied the city, bringing the disorder under control at last.

The riots left many neighborhoods in ruins. Washingtonians staggered under the shock of what had happened. A group of teachers in a mostly black area around Fourteenth Street collected the comments of their students in a poignant booklet. One fourth-grader stated simply, "Washington wasn't Washington last week."

Over the following years, the District of Columbia made major strides toward representation in national and local government. In

On January 2, 1975, Walter Washington was sworn in as the first elected mayor of Washington in more than one hundred years.

1970, Washingtonians regained the right to elect a delegate to the United States House of Representatives—a right they had lost in 1874. The District representative has a voting voice in House committees, but is not entitled to participate in full House votes.

In 1973, Congress finally approved a mayor-council form of government for Washington. For the first time in one hundred years, Washingtonians held a mayoral election in 1974. As their city's leader, they chose a black candidate named Walter E. Washington, who had previously served as city commissioner.

Washingtonians had made real gains toward representative government, but many were still unhappy with their ambiguous status. In a 1980 referendum, a majority of Washington's citizens voted to apply for statehood. As United States territories had done in the past, Washington held a constitutional convention and drew up a code of laws for the proposed state of New Columbia. Washington voters accepted the state constitution late in 1982, and sent it to Congress for final approval. No vote was ever taken in Congress, and the statehood issue remains in limbo.

During the 1980s, Washington suffered the same social problems that plagued other American cities—poverty, drug

In historic Washington, the problems of modern life "are being attacked with zeal and courage."

abuse, and a rising crime rate. By 1989, gang warfare turned some neighborhoods into battlefields. Early in 1990, Mayor Marion Barry was arrested for possession of cocaine. In Washington—the national capital and a leader in the international community— such problems seem especially tragic.

Edward Brooke grew up in an integrated neighborhood in Northwest Washington. After going away to study and launch his career in Massachusetts, he returned in 1967, the first black United States senator to serve in the twentieth century. In Washington, Brooke saw reflected the problems of the nation as a whole, and wrote: "Our true adversaries are the circumstances that lead to our national ills . . . the deterioration of our cities and our countryside, the continuing threat of war, the accumulation of racial and religious resentments, and the pent-up aspirations caused by what we think of as progress. . . . They are the problems that fill the docks of the Congress and cause lights to burn late in the administrative offices of the government of the United States. There is no avoiding them, and it is exciting to feel that here they are being attacked with zeal and courage."

63

Chapter 7

GOVERNMENT AND THE ECONOMY

GOVERNMENT AND THE ECONOMY

GOVERNMENT

As the nation's capital, Washington has a unique relationship
with the federal government. Since 1974, the city has operated
under a mayor-council form of government. Most offices of the
city government are located in the District Building at Fourteenth
Street and Pennsylvania Avenue.

Washington's mayor, who is elected to a four-year term,
appoints the heads of such departments as sanitation and law
enforcement. The mayor prepares the city budget, and may
propose laws to the city council.

Washington is divided into eight electoral districts. Each of
these districts elects one member of the city council, and five more
members are chosen at large in a citywide election. Although the
council votes on local laws, its decisions must be approved by the
United States Congress. The mayor's budget must meet not only
the approval of the city council, but also the approval of Congress
and the president.

About 60 percent of the property in Washington is tax free,
belonging to the federal government or to foreign embassies.
Nevertheless, the city generates about two-thirds of its revenue
through property, sales, and income taxes. The rest of the city's
funds come from the federal government. Despite the federal
government's contribution, residents and property owners in
Washington are among the most heavily taxed people in the
United States.

Among Washington's institutions of higher learning are George Washington University (above) and American University (right).

EDUCATION

One of the biggest items in Washington's budget is education. More than 87,000 students attend Washington's public elementary and secondary schools. Some 25,000 more students are enrolled in eighty private schools.

Washington is home to seventeen institutions of higher learning. The University of the District of Columbia (UDC), founded in 1976, has three campuses in the city. The Catholic University of America is the national university of the Roman Catholic Church. Howard University, created by the Freedmen's Bureau in 1867, is the most prominent black university in the nation. Other leading schools in the capital include Georgetown University, American University, and George Washington University. Established in 1864, Gallaudet University is the only college in the world created for students who are deaf, conducting all of its classes in sign language.

The Washington subway system, known as the Metro, crisscrosses the city and fans out into many nearby towns.

TRANSPORTATION AND COMMUNICATION

Every day, hundreds of thousands of people in Washington and its sprawling metropolitan area take to the highways, commuting by automobile to their jobs. The Capital Beltway loops around the city and links it with suburbs in Maryland and Virginia. Despite the complex highway system, however, Washington commuters spend uncounted hours each year caught in traffic jams.

Washington's public transportation system helps to ease the traffic strain. The Washington Area Metropolitan Transit Authority operates an extensive bus service throughout the city and many of its suburbs. The first section of Washington's subway system, known locally as the Metro, opened in 1976. The system's five lines crisscross the city and fan out into many nearby towns. Cars on the Metro are clean and carpeted, with comfortable cushioned seats, putting many other American subway systems to shame.

Washington is served by three major airports. Washington National Airport and Dulles International Airport are on the

Dulles International Airport is one of three major airports that serve Washington.

other side of the Potomac in Virginia. Baltimore-Washington International Airport (BWI) is located in Friendship, Maryland.

Fourteen television stations and more than forty radio stations serve Washington and its metropolitan area. The capital's major newspaper is the nationally respected *Washington Post*. Numerous other publications originate in Washington, including *National Geographic*, *U.S. News & World Report*, *The Nation*, and *The New Republic*. Thousands of publications, from leaflets to scholarly monographs, are produced by the federal government in Washington each year. Government publications cover virtually every topic known to man, from archaeology to Zimbabwe.

ECONOMY

Unlike most major American cities, Washington has never developed as a center for manufacturing and trade. Its economy rests almost entirely on the vast complex of offices that comprises the federal government. The government provides jobs for about 374,000 men and women in the Washington, D.C., metropolitan

In the course of a year, tourists outnumber permanent residents almost twelve to one.

area. The government employs janitors, secretaries, researchers, attorneys, writers, elected officials, and workers in hundreds of other occupations.

The presence of the federal government draws corporations, labor organizations, conservation societies, and many other special-interest groups to the capital. From this vantage point, they can "lobby" government officials—that is, try to persuade them to act in ways that will meet their organization's needs.

Apart from the government itself, the most essential ingredient in Washington's economy is tourism. An estimated 10 million visitors flock to Washington each year—to tour the White House, the Capitol, and the Smithsonian; to gaze at the monuments; and to walk the streets where so much history has taken shape. In the course of a year, tourists outnumber permanent residents almost twelve to one. A good tourist season brings boom times to Washington's hotels, restaurants, and shopping centers. As long as Washington is the nation's seat of power, it will be a magnet for people who want to see the places they have heard about, to take in the city's unique atmosphere, to marvel and to wonder.

Chapter 8

CULTURE AND ENTERTAINMENT

Minerals and Gems

Earth, Moon and Meteorites

Fossil Plants and Animals

CULTURE AND ENTERTAINMENT

The federal government, with its focus on political issues and international policy, is the hub around which Washington revolves. Yet the nation's capital is also one of the finest places in the world to view artistic masterpieces or to hear outstanding musical performances. Throughout its history, Washington has nurtured acclaimed artists, writers, and composers. Today, the capital also hosts leading college and professional sports teams. In athletics and in every field of creative endeavor, Washington has made major contributions to American culture.

LITERATURE

In 1807, Joel Barlow, a friend of Thomas Jefferson, settled at Kalorama, a large estate near Rock Creek. Barlow was one of the leading intellectuals of his day—a lawyer, a diplomat, and a philosopher as well as a poet. During his stay in Washington, he published his best-known work, *The Columbiad*, an epic that traced the history of America.

Late in 1861, Julia Ward Howe, a visitor from Boston, observed a review of Union troops outside Washington. That night, she returned to her lodgings at Willard's Hotel and wrote a stirring poem that began: "Mine eyes have seen the glory of the coming of the Lord. . . . " Set to the tune of a popular song, her "Battle Hymn of the Republic" became a favorite Union marching song throughout the Civil War, and remains one of the nation's most cherished ballads today.

Walt Whitman (left), who lived in Washington from 1862 to 1873, is considered one of America's greatest poets. Author Frances Hodgson Burnett (right), the center of a lively social and literary circle, wrote the popular novel *Little Lord Fauntleroy*.

Counted among the greatest poets America has ever produced, Walt Whitman lived and worked in Washington between 1862 and 1873. During the Civil War, he volunteered as a nurse in Washington's many makeshift hospitals. When the war was over, he remained in the capital, working as a clerk in various government offices. The unrhymed "free verse" of Whitman's most famous poetry collection, *Leaves of Grass*, shocked the literary establishment of his time, but today Whitman is considered the father of modern poetry. While he lived in Washington, Whitman wrote two of his best-known poems, "When Lilacs Last in the Dooryard Bloom'd" and "O Captain, My Captain," both tributes to Abraham Lincoln.

Grandson of President John Quincy Adams, Henry Adams first visited Washington when he was twelve years old. After traveling in Europe and the United States, he finally settled in the capital in 1877. Adams's novel *Democracy*, which appeared in 1880, depicts life in Washington after the Civil War. *The Education of Henry Adams*, published shortly after the author's death in 1918, is regarded by critics as one of the finest autobiographies ever written. Adams also wrote several biographies and a history of medieval France, *Mont-Saint-Michel and Chartres*. His home on Lafayette Square was a center for literary and intellectual life in the capital.

Like Henry Adams, Frances Hodgson Burnett became the center of a lively social and literary circle. Her 1883 novel *Through One Administration* exposed corruption in Washington politics. The most popular of her more than forty novels was *Little Lord Fauntleroy*, published in 1886. It is the story of an American boy who suddenly inherits a title and an estate in England.

Adams's *Democracy* and Burnett's *Through One Administration* were the forerunners of a fictional genre that gathered momentum in the twentieth century, the "Washington novel." In such works as Allen Drury's *Advise and Consent*, Fletcher Knebel's *Seven Days in May*, and Ward Just's *Honor, Power, Riches, Fame, and The Love of Women*, authors revealed the machinations of Washington's power brokers.

These contemporary novels focus on elegant Georgetown mansions and the halls of the Capitol, paying almost no attention to the other Washington—the home of thousands of black families who struggle in poverty. The publication of Marita Golden's *Long Distance Ride* in 1989 began to fill this gap. In this vivid novel about four generations of a black family, Golden portrays Washington from the point of view of some of its black citizens.

ART

Washington's galleries and museums house extraordinary treasures of art from every period of civilization and from every nation on earth. In addition, Washington itself and the notable people who live there have inspired countless artists whose work is displayed throughout the city.

73

John Trumbull's huge painting *The Declaration of Independence, July 4, 1776* **hangs in the Capitol Rotunda along with seven other historical paintings.**

In the early days of the Republic, the finest artists in America adorned the capital with paintings that reflected their patriotic zeal. Gilbert Stuart and Charles Willson Peale painted heroic portraits of George Washington. John Trumbull created historic panels in the Capitol Rotunda, including *The Declaration of Independence, July 4, 1776; Surrender of Cornwallis;* and *Washington Resigning His Commission as Commander-in-Chief of the Army.*

Among the statues in the Capitol Rotunda are bronze likenesses of Thomas Jefferson and Benjamin Franklin by Hiram Powers. Clark Mills's statue of Andrew Jackson, which graces Lafayette Square, was the first large-scale equestrian sculpture ever created in the United States.

Many European artists contributed paintings and sculpture to the capital. The works of Giuseppe Franzoni, Enrico Causici, Antonio Capellano, and several other Italian sculptors adorn many of Washington's public buildings. French sculptor Nicholas Gevelot designed *Penn's Treaty with the Indians,* a relief over the west entrance to the Capitol.

The Brumidi Corridor (left), in the Senate wing of the Capitol, was decorated with colorful birds, animals, flowers, fruit, and scrollwork. Clark Mills's statue of Andrew Jackson, on Lafayette Square, was the first large equestrian statue ever created in the United States.

A victim of political persecution at home, Italian painter Constantino Brumidi arrived in Washington in 1852. He once explained that he was determined "to make beautiful the capital of the one country on earth where there is liberty." For almost twenty-five years, Brumidi created panoramic frescoes within the Capitol. His *Apotheosis of George Washington* encircles the inner dome of the Capitol Rotunda. In 1879, when the painter was in his mid-seventies, his chair slipped from the scaffold where he was working. Fortunately, he managed to hang onto a ladder 180 feet (55 meters) above the Rotunda floor for fifteen minutes until help arrived. Brumidi always signed his paintings, "C. Brumidi, Artist, Citizen of the United States."

Washington's parks and intersections are sprinkled with statues, many of them dating from the nineteenth century. Augustus Saint-Gaudens's *Adams Memorial* stands in Rock Creek Park. A group of buffaloes by A. Phimister Proctor greets commuters at the Q Street Bridge. Gutzon Borglum's figure of General Philip H. Sheridan on horseback prances in Sheridan Circle. The graceful Dupont Memorial Fountain in Dupont Circle is the work of Daniel Chester French, who is best known for his seated statue of Abraham Lincoln at the Lincoln Memorial.

In the twentieth century, art in Washington turned toward realism, depicting the day-to-day lives of ordinary people. Doris Lee's *Mail Box at the Crossroads* was created for the Post Office Department Building, and the Interior Building boasts William Gropper's painting *The Construction of a Dam*.

More recent artwork in the capital reflects the modern trend toward abstract expressionism. The Corcoran Gallery of Art hosts biennial exhibitions of paintings and sculpture by some of the nation's most innovative contemporary artists.

PERFORMING ARTS

Music in all its forms—from rock to classical—flourishes in Washington, D.C. The Smithsonian Institution sponsors performances of traditional music from around the world. Classical concerts on original period instruments can be heard at the Library of Congress and the Folger Shakespeare Library. The National Symphony Orchestra, founded in 1931, plays regularly at the John F. Kennedy Center Concert Hall. Internationally acclaimed orchestras and companies are scheduled throughout the year at the John F. Kennedy Center for the Performing Arts.

The Marine Band, once led by John Philip Sousa, performing on the White House grounds

In 1798, an act of Congress established the Marine Band, which is still based in Washington. Nicknamed "The President's Own," the Marine Band has performed at every presidential inauguration since 1801. The band's most outstanding leader was John Philip Sousa, who presided from 1880 until 1892. Sometimes called the "March King," Sousa composed such stirring marches as "The Washington Post," "Semper Fidelis," and "The Stars and Stripes Forever."

Washington attracts visiting repertory companies from all over the country, and nurtures several theatrical groups of its own. The Arena Stage at Sixth and M streets in Southwest Washington was founded in 1961 as the home of the Arena Repertory Company. The Eisenhower Theater at the Kennedy Center is the largest legitimate theater in the capital, with a seating capacity of eleven thousand.

Ford's Theatre, where Abraham Lincoln was assassinated, has been fully restored.

Ford's Theatre, on Tenth Street, NW, shut its doors to the public in 1865 after John Wilkes Booth shot Abraham Lincoln during a performance of a comedy called *Our American Cousin*. It has been fully restored by the National Park Service to its appearance on that night, and it reopened in 1968.

SPORTS

Basketball—the city game—is the most popular team sport in the nation's capital. It is played in schoolyards, in neighborhood gyms, and in back alleys. Basketball fans follow the exploits of Georgetown University. For decades, Georgetown had little basketball prowess. Then the university hired coach John Thompson, who recruited hardworking and talented players from the inner cities, and the school became a powerhouse. Led by domineering center Patrick Ewing, Georgetown won a national championship in 1984.

The National Football League Washington Redskins play football in Robert F. Kennedy (RFK) Stadium.

Fans of professional basketball follow the Washington Bullets of the NBA and hockey aficionados watch the Washington Capitals. Both teams play their home games in nearby Landover, Maryland.

Until 1971, Washington had a baseball team—the Senators. Year after year, the president of the United States would attend the opening Senators game, throw out the first pitch, and officially launch a new baseball season. Over the years, the Senators produced excellent players such as Hall of Fame pitcher Walter Johnson and sharp-hitting first baseman Mickey Vernon. But the team won only three pennants in the seventy-year history of baseball in Washington. The Senators' performance was so dismal that nightclub comics quipped: "Washington—first in war, first in peace, last in the American League."

Certainly no losers are the Washington Redskins of the National Football League. With players such as Sonny Jurgensen in the 1960s and 1970s, and Joe Thiesmann, Larry Brown, and Doug Williams in the 1980s, the Redskins are one of the most feared teams in pro football. In 1987, Doug Williams became the first black quarterback to lead his team to a Super Bowl victory.

Chapter 9
A VISIT TO WASHINGTON

A VISIT TO WASHINGTON

It has sometimes been said that Washington, D.C., has three faces. It is the nation's administrative capital and a center for international affairs. It is also a repository of America's cultural and historical heritage. And it is a major urban center, home to more than half a million people. Visitors should experience all of these aspects in order to understand this great and unique city.

THE PRESIDENT'S NEIGHBORHOOD

The section of the city that lies north of the Mall and west of North Capitol Street is referred to as Northwest Washington. The Northwest is the largest part of the city, comprising almost half its area. Nearly 50 percent of all Washingtonians live in the Northwest.

The most famous resident of Northwest Washington is the president of the United States, who lives at 1600 Pennsylvania Avenue. The president's home, which was officially named the White House by Theodore Roosevelt, sometimes receives as many as ten thousand visitors in a single day. The White House has 132 rooms and 20 baths. Thomas Jefferson once said it was "big enough for two emperors, one pope, and a grand lama."

Among the rooms that are open to the public is the magnificent East Room, 80 feet (24 meters) long with an 18-foot (5-meter)

Among the elegant White House rooms that are open to the public is the Green Room.

ceiling. On one wall hangs Gilbert Stuart's great unfinished portrait of George Washington, which Dolley Madison rescued when the British set fire to the White House in 1814. Abraham Lincoln, John F. Kennedy, and five other presidents who died in office were laid in state in the East Room.

Visitors may also tour the Green Room, the Red Room, the Blue Room, and the State Dining Room. The State Dining Room can seat up to 140 guests at formal banquets. Above the fireplace hangs a full-length portrait of Abraham Lincoln. On the mantelpiece is inscribed a quotation from John Adams's famous letter to his wife, invoking blessings on all who live in the house.

Just south of the White House lies an oval park called the Ellipse. The Ellipse hosts band concerts on warm evenings, and softball games throughout the spring and summer. Lafayette

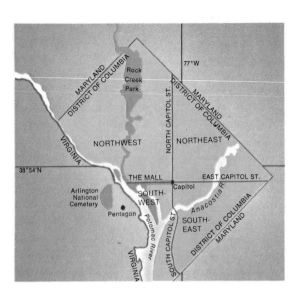

One of the two great bronze
lions that guard the entrance
to the Corcoran Gallery of Art

Square is north of the White House, across Pennsylvania Avenue.
The square's centerpiece is the equestrian statue of Andrew
Jackson, which sculptor Clark Mills made with bronze from
British cannons captured by Jackson in the War of 1812.

Two blocks west of the White House stands the Octagon House,
which served as the president's home between 1814 and 1819.
According to legend, the Octagon House and the White House
were once joined by a secret underground tunnel that led all the
way to the Potomac River. In time of danger, the story runs, the
president could escape to a waiting boat.

The entrance to the Corcoran Gallery of Art is guarded by two
great bronze lions. The Corcoran displays a priceless collection of
American masterpieces, including two Gilbert Stuart portraits of
George Washington.

A museum at the national headquarters of the American Red Cross traces the history of the organization.

Not far from the Corcoran is the national headquarters of the American Red Cross. A museum traces the history of the organization, even preserving a battered ambulance from World War I. At the nearby headquarters of the Daughters of the American Revolution (DAR), visitors can search out their roots in one of the most extensive genealogical libraries in the world.

The Naval Observatory at Massachusetts Avenue and Thirty-fourth Street was constructed over an old soapstone quarry once used by the Piscataway Indians. The observatory conducts astronomical studies and sets standard time for the United States. Since 1968, the official home of the vice-president has been located on the observatory grounds.

Northeast of the White House stands Ford's Theatre, where Abraham Lincoln was shot in 1865. Today, Ford's Theatre contains a collection of mementos relating to Lincoln's life and death, including several of his law books, items from the 1864 presidential campaign, and newspaper accounts of the assassination and later conspiracy trial. Furniture from Lincoln's

Murals enliven the buildings of the Adams-Morgan neighborhood.

home in Springfield, Illinois, is on display across the street at Petersen House, where the president died.

NORTHWEST WASHINGTON

About a mile north of the White House is the colorful Adams-Morgan neighborhood, a spicy ethnic blend of Latin American and Southeast Asian cultures. Sweeping freehand murals enliven the walls of the buildings. People from all over the D.C. area flock to Adams-Morgan's farmers' market on Saturday mornings.

From north to south through Northwest Washington winds the 1,800-acre (728-hectare) Rock Creek Park, the largest park in the city. Much of the park is densely wooded, threaded with hiking trails and bicycle paths. President Theodore Roosevelt used to delight in leading visiting dignitaries on vigorous walks through

Historic row houses line many of Georgetown's streets.

the park, usually leaving his guests thoroughly winded. Near the park's Connecticut Avenue entrance is the National Zoological Park, which houses twenty-five hundred birds, mammals, and reptiles representing six hundred species.

One of the finest of Washington's many art museums is the Phillips Collection at Massachusetts Avenue and Twenty-first Street. In this pleasant, informal setting visitors may sit on sofas and admire works by Van Gogh, Klee, Renoir, Picasso, and other masters at their leisure.

Once a thriving port on the Potomac, Georgetown retains much of its nineteenth-century charm. Some of its narrow, tree-lined streets are still cobbled, and its Federal and Georgian homes are a delight to students of architecture. Among Georgetown's most outstanding historic homes is Laird-Dunlap House, which once belonged to Abraham Lincoln's son, Robert Todd Lincoln.

Dumbarton Oaks is now a museum displaying Byzantine jewelry and pre-Columbian art.

Dumbarton Oaks, the scene of the 1944 conference that led to the United Nations Charter, is now a museum displaying Byzantine jewelry and pre-Columbian art.

The John F. Kennedy Center for the Performing Arts opened in 1971 with a world premier performance of Leonard Bernstein's *Mass* in the Opera House. In addition to the Opera House, the JFK Center contains the Eisenhower Theater, the Concert Hall, and the American Film Institute Theater. A bronze head of Kennedy dominates the Grand Foyer.

North of the Kennedy Center is the celebrated Watergate Complex, a cluster of high-rise apartments, office buildings, and a hotel that made international headlines in the early 1970s. During the 1972 presidential campaign, burglars broke into Democratic headquarters at the Watergate to uncover campaign strategies. Scandals surrounding the Watergate affair eventually led to the resignation of President Richard M. Nixon.

The John F. Kennedy Center for the Performing Arts

SOUTH OF THE MALL

Southwest Washington (south of the Mall and west of South Capitol Street) comprises only about one-eighth of the city's area. About 4 percent of all Washingtonians live in this tiny section. In the 1950s, a massive urban-renewal project razed blocks of squalid slums in the Southwest, replacing them with modern apartments and office buildings. Many government offices are located here, including the Department of Agriculture and the Department of Transportation.

Southeast Washington (east of South Capitol Street) is largely a residential section, containing some of Washington's wealthiest homes as well as some of its poorest. Anacostia, the sprawling neighborhood south of the Anacostia River, includes the Historic District and Cedar Hill.

Cedar Hill, the Frederick Douglass Memorial Home, stands on the crest of a hill at Fourteenth and W Streets, SE. The home of the eloquent black abolitionist from 1889 to 1895, Cedar Hill houses an extensive collection of Douglass's papers, furniture, and other memorabilia. By tradition, Washington schoolchildren visit Cedar Hill for an annual memorial service on February 14, Douglass's birthday.

The Anacostia Neighborhood Museum operates under the auspices of the Smithsonian Institution. Exhibits focus on African history and on the history of black people in the United States. The museum sponsors many educational programs, including classes in dance, art, music, and drama.

NORTHEAST WASHINGTON

Northeast Washington lies between North Capitol and East Capitol streets, comprising about one-fourth of the city. It is largely a residential section, providing both middle-income and low-income housing. At the northern end of this section spreads the National Arboretum, an experimental forest preserve. Encompassing many types of terrain from hills to marshland, the Arboretum is a setting for a wide variety of exotic trees and plants, as well as many that are native to the D.C. area. Nearby, the Kenilworth Aquatic Gardens display many fascinating and beautiful plants that grow in water.

Many leading Roman Catholic shrines are located in Northeast Washington, including Mount Olivet Cemetery, the Franciscan Monastery Memorial Church of the Holy Land, and the Shrine of the Immaculate Conception. Also in Northeast Washington stands the Catholic University of America, the only school in the United States that receives the direct patronage of the pope.

Cedar Hill, the Frederick Douglass Memorial Home

Another unique institution in Northeast Washington is
Gallaudet University, the only college in the world for the
education of deaf students. In 1988, Gallaudet made the front
pages when students demanded and won the appointment of a
deaf president. I. King Jordan became the first deaf person to
serve as president since the school's founding in 1864.

On the north bank of the Anacostia lies the Congressional
Cemetery, the final resting place of many congressmen who died
in office between 1807 and 1886. Regarding the grim monuments
that mark most of the graves, a Massachusetts representative once
remarked, "To be buried beneath one of these formidable objects
would add a new terror to death." In addition to congressmen, the
cemetery contains the graves of such other notable people as
composer John Philip Sousa, architect Robert Mills, and
Pushmataha, a Choctaw Indian chief.

Chapter 10

CAPITOL HILL
AND THE
MALL

CAPITOL HILL AND THE MALL

According to Pierre-Charles L'Enfant's plan, the United States Capitol was to be at Washington's geographic center. An open mall running west from the Capitol was to lead directly to a grand monument dedicated to George Washington. On the map, Capitol Hill is no longer the center of Washington. Due to the marshy ground, the Washington Monument was not built on the precise spot L'Enfant selected. But, as he envisioned, Capitol Hill and the Mall, with their government buildings and monuments, are the spiritual heart of the nation's capital.

ON CAPITOL HILL

The United States Capitol is an immense, stately structure on 16 acres (6 hectares) of grounds. Like a city in miniature, it has its own post office, first-aid station, beauty salons, library, machine repair shops, and printing offices. More than 19,000 men and women work in the Capitol, assisting the nation's 540 members of Congress.

Nearly every president since Andrew Jackson has been inaugurated on the steps that lead to the Capitol's east entrance. Two enormous bronze doors lead into the Capitol Rotunda, a vast circular room 100 feet (30 meters) across and 180 feet (55 meters) high. The Rotunda is adorned with statues, paintings, and frescoes

Brumidi's *Apotheosis of George Washington* encircles the domed ceiling of the Capitol Rotunda. Nearby Statuary Hall contains statues honoring each state's most famous citizen.

representing people and events from American history. Visitors can view John Chapman's *Baptism of Pocahontas*, John Trumbull's *Surrender of Cornwallis*, and the marble figure of Lincoln carved by seventeen-year-old Vinnie Ream shortly after Lincoln's death. Brumidi's *Apotheosis of George Washington* encircles the dome-shaped ceiling high above. The 9-million-ton (8-million-metric-ton) cast-iron dome is crowned by Thomas Crawford's statue *Freedom*.

Down a short corridor from the Rotunda is Statuary Hall, where the various states of the Union honor their most famous

The Rayburn Building (left) is one of three House office buildings. The Supreme Court (right) was designed by architect Cass Gilbert.

citizens in bronze and marble. The statues have overflowed Statuary Hall and spilled out into the corridor. Just outside the door is the figure of humorist Will Rogers, who once remarked, "When the politicians get serious, it's then that they do such amusing things."

According to tradition, Republican representatives sit to the speaker's left and Democrats to the speaker's right in the House and Senate chambers. Both chambers have visitors' galleries from which the public can observe the proceedings.

A network of tunnels connects the Capitol to the office buildings in which much of the legislature's business is conducted. Senators use the Russell, Dirksen, and Hart buildings, and representatives use the Rayburn, Longworth, and Cannon House office buildings.

A double row of Corinthian columns, made from Vermont marble, gives the Supreme Court the air of an ancient Greek

The elaborate Neoclassical Library of Congress is a vast treasure house containing 84 million items, including a Gutenberg Bible printed in the 1450s.

temple. Completed in 1935, the Court building was designed by architect Cass Gilbert, who is believed to have coined its motto, "Equal Justice under Law." Visitors may attend sessions in the red-draped Court Chamber, where the nine justices sit on a long bench and hand down decisions that may affect any aspect of American life.

South of the Supreme Court stand the three buildings that comprise the Library of Congress. Created in 1800 as an information resource for congressmen, the library today is a vast treasure house of books and pamphlets; newspapers, magazines and journals; maps and manuscripts; films, photographs, recordings, and sheet music—some 84 million items in all. Among the library's most fascinating exhibits are a Gutenberg Bible printed in the 1450s, an original version of the Gettysburg

The United States Botanic Garden, at the southwestern edge of the Capitol grounds

Address, and a collection of photographs taken during the Civil War.

Nearby, the Folger Shakespeare Library houses a collection of works by and about the English playwright, including many rare manuscripts. The stacks are open only to scholars, but the public may attend plays, concerts, and poetry readings sponsored by the library. Shakespeare enthusiasts enjoy exploring a replica of an Elizabethan theater.

The United States Botanic Garden is an oasis of peace at the southwestern edge of the Capitol grounds. Its greenhouses and outdoor gardens display more than ten thousand varieties of plants and shrubs.

THE FEDERAL TRIANGLE

West of Capitol Hill is a long, grassy strip of land called the Mall, bounded by Independence Avenue to the south and

On permanent display in the main hall of the National Archives Building are the original Declaration of Independence and the Constitution.

Constitution Avenue to the north. Along the northern edge of the Mall, on a long, narrow triangle formed by Constitution Avenue, Pennsylvania Avenue, and Fifteenth Street, stand a group of massive limestone buildings with red-tiled roofs. These government structures are the buildings of the Federal Triangle.

Marking the eastern point of the triangle at Sixth Street, the Andrew Mellon Memorial Fountain was dedicated in 1952. The Apex Building, which stands on a triangular plot between Sixth and Seventh streets, houses the Federal Trade Commission. The National Archives Building, just to the west, is an impressive example of classic architecture, with stately colonnades and porticoes. On permanent display in the main hall are the original Declaration of Independence and the Constitution. In time of emergency, these priceless documents can be automatically lowered to a vault beneath the building.

Among the city's most interesting places to visit is the Federal Bureau of Investigation, whose new building lies across from the

Federal Triangle on Pennsylvania Avenue. Exhibits at the FBI laboratory show how investigators use tiny samples of hair, blood, metal, and other substances in unraveling crimes. Visitors are invited to watch FBI agents practice at the shooting range.

Billions of dollars in federal taxes are collected each year under the auspices of the Internal Revenue Service, housed in an imposing square building with 1,750 offices. Next door, the clock tower of the Old Post Office Building juts above the otherwise level row of rooftops. Constructed in 1890, the Old Post Office was superseded in 1934 by the adjoining Post Office Department Building. The Stamp Exhibition Room in the Post Office Department Building displays every stamp issued by the department since 1847. Inside the entrance on Pennsylvania Avenue stands a bronze statue of Benjamin Franklin, the founder of the United States postal system.

The six-story marble District Building is Washington's City Hall. A series of plaques on the walls of the entrance vestibule commemorate Washington's former commissioners.

Other buildings in the Federal Triangle house the Department of Justice, the Department of Labor, and the Department of Commerce. Exhibits in all of these buildings give the public a glimpse into the complex workings of the federal government.

THE NATION'S ATTIC

In the spirit with which it was founded, for the "increase and diffusion of knowledge among men," the Smithsonian Institution today encompasses fourteen museums and galleries, five research facilities, and a zoo (the National Zoological Park in Rock Creek Park). Its buildings preserve millions of items of scientific, artistic, and historic value, from African beetles to satellites. It is no

The Smithsonian's oldest building, known as the Castle, opened in 1852.

wonder that writer Mark Twain once referred to the Smithsonian as the "nation's attic."

The Smithsonian's oldest building, known as the Castle because of its ornate towers, opened in 1852. Today, it is used chiefly for administrative offices and information services. The tomb of the Smithsonian's benefactor, James Smithson, is located in the Castle's North Foyer.

The two newest museums in the Smithsonian complex, both of them composed of underground galleries, are entered through pavilions in the Victorian garden behind the Castle. The Arthur M. Sackler Gallery features the art of Asia, including a broad range of contemporary work. The National Museum of African Art specializes in traditional art of Africa south of the Sahara. This museum offers extensive programs for children in the Washington area.

The Freer Gallery, just south of the Castle, was donated in 1906 by Charles Lang Freer, a Detroit industrialist. The Freer contains outstanding collections of Far Eastern and Middle Eastern paintings, pottery, jade, and porcelain. Its American galleries include works by such masters as Winslow Homer, John Singer Sargent, and Augustus Saint-Gaudens.

The Arts and Industries Museum displays a unique assortment of objects originally collected for the nation's Centennial Exposition, which was held in Philadelphia in 1876. The exhibits reflect America's pride in the technological achievements of its first hundred years. They include steam-powered pumps, hand-operated printing presses, a 42-foot (13-meter) model of the naval cruiser *Antietam*, and a giant refrigeration compressor. In the style of the era, many of the machines are adorned with pictures of eagles, grapes, or flowers.

The Hirshhorn Museum and Sculpture Garden specializes in artistic works of the past two centuries. The modernistic, circular building holds sculptures and paintings by such European masters as Rodin and Picasso, and by Americans such as Alexander Calder, Mary Cassatt, and Jackson Pollock. An additional seventy-five pieces of sculpture are scattered through the 1.3-acre (0.5-hectare) Sculpture Garden.

Exhibits at the National Air and Space Museum trace the history of manned flight and space exploration. The twenty-four galleries display spacecraft, missiles and rockets, and aircraft of historical or technological importance. In addition there are hundreds of scale models, uniforms, aviation awards, photographs, and other memorabilia. The museum's collection includes the plane flown by the Wright brothers at Kitty Hawk, North Carolina, in 1903; the *Spirit of St. Louis*, in which Charles Lindbergh crossed the Atlantic Ocean alone in 1927; and the

Among the many museums, galleries, research parks, and other establishments maintained by the Smithsonian Institution are (clockwise from above) the National Zoological Park, the National Gallery of Art, the National Air and Space Museum, and the National Museum of Natural History.

command module from *Apollo 11*, which carried human beings to the moon for the first time in 1969.

On the north side of the Mall stands the National Gallery of Art, presenting masterworks by both American and European painters. The National Gallery also maintains its own orchestra.

At the National Museum of Natural History, visitors are overwhelmed by an array of exhibits on every aspect of the natural world, from rocks to rain forests. On the ground floor, a series of vivid murals called *Our Changing Land* depicts the Washington, D.C., area as it was transformed from woodland and swamp to a landscape of roads and bridges. One of the most popular items to be seen is the dazzling Hope Diamond in the Hall of Minerals, said to have brought misfortune to each of its owners. Other displays cover ancient reptiles, mammals in their natural environment, the evolution of man, and native cultures from around the world.

In the main hall on the ground floor of the National Museum of History and Technology hangs one of the nation's treasures—the enormous American flag that inspired "The Star-Spangled Banner." The museum's exhibits celebrate the extraordinary richness of American history. Visitors can marvel at a printing press once used by Benjamin Franklin, Eli Whitney's cotton gin, and a stunning collection of gowns worn by America's First Ladies. Other exhibits trace the development of clothing, farm machinery, vehicles, bridges and tunnels, clocks, and computers. In the Hall of Medical Science is a set of George Washington's false teeth, made of gold and ivory. An exhibit called "A Nation of Nations" honors the diverse peoples who explored and settled the United States.

The Smithsonian Institution also maintains several museums off the Mall. The National Museum of American Art at G and Eighth streets has a fine collection of American painting and sculpture, excellent facilities for scholarly research, and an Explore Gallery for children. The National Portrait Gallery was established in 1962 by an act of Congress to collect and exhibit portraits of "men and women who have made significant contributions to the history, development, and culture of the people of the United States." The Renwick Gallery, a block from the White House on Pennsylvania Avenue, has special exhibits on American design and crafts.

THE GRAND MONUMENTS

No other attraction in Washington draws more visitors than the Lincoln Memorial, which stands on the bank of the Potomac River. The monument's design resembles that of the Parthenon of ancient Athens. Its thirty-six columns represent the thirty-six stars that appeared in the Union flag when Lincoln died. In the monument's inner chamber is Daniel Chester French's famous statue of the sixteenth president, brooding over the city with bowed head. Lincoln's second inaugural speech and his Gettysburg Address are engraved on the interior walls.

The Lincoln Memorial has long been a symbol of freedom. In 1939, after she had been denied the chance to perform at Constitution Hall because of her race, black contralto Marian Anderson sang here to an audience of seventy-five thousand people. In 1963, Dr. Martin Luther King, Jr., delivered his stirring "I have a dream" speech at this shrine to equal rights for all Americans.

Overlooking the Tidal Basin, the Jefferson Memorial was dedicated in 1943 on the two hundredth anniversary of Thomas Jefferson's birth. The domed structure, surrounded by twenty-six Ionic columns, is made of Indiana limestone. Quotations from the

The Lincoln Memorial

Declaration of Independence and several of Jefferson's other writings are inscribed on the inner walls, surrounding a statue of the third president.

The design for the Vietnam Veterans Memorial was submitted in a contest by Maya Ying Lin, a twenty-one-year-old student at Yale University. On a V-shaped wall of black granite are inscribed the names of all the American servicemen and servicewomen who died or were declared missing in action in Southeast Asia between 1959 and 1975. On the grounds stands a statue of three soldiers, one white, one black, and one Hispanic. Each year, thousands of Vietnam survivors, as well as parents, widows, children, and friends of those who died, make the pilgrimage to this monument

Above: The Thomas Jefferson statue in the Jefferson Memorial Right: The Washington Monument

and search for the names of their loved ones. Many people consider the Vietnam Veterans Memorial the most beautiful and moving monument in all of Washington. Ironically, Maya Ying Lin received only a B-minus for the design from her art professor at Yale.

The only monument on the Mall that was specifically planned by Pierre-Charles L'Enfant is the Washington Monument, which stands almost midway between the White House and the Jefferson Memorial. A marble obelisk 555 feet (169 meters) high, the Washington Monument is the highest masonry structure in the world. The monument was designed by architect Robert Mills and

A young man makes a rubbing of a name at the Vietnam Veterans Memorial in Constitution Gardens.

dedicated in 1878. Around the base flutter fifty flags, one for each state in the Union.

From the observation deck that crowns the Washington Monument, visitors can see the White House to the north, the Lincoln Memorial on the Potomac River to the west, the Jefferson Memorial to the south, and to the east, the Mall leading to the Capitol. Perhaps L'Enfant pictured this splendid panorama when he planned his city of boulevards, parks, and statues. The view from the Washington Monument is a stirring reminder of the democratic ideals on which the city was founded to serve as the capital of the United States of America.

FACTS AT A GLANCE

GENERAL INFORMATION

Federal District: Since December 1, 1800

Origin of Name: Washington, the city that makes up the entire District of Columbia, was named for the nation's first president, George Washington.

Nicknames: "Nation's Capital," "A Capital City"

Flag: Three red stars above two horizontal red stripes on a white field.

Motto: *Jutitia Omnibus* (Justice for All)

District Flower: American beauty rose

District Bird: Wood thrush

District Tree: Scarlet oak

POPULATION

Population: 638,432

Population Density: 9,253 people per sq. mi. (3,567 people per km^2)

Population Growth: The District of Columbia grew slowly but steadily in the early 1800s, followed by a major spurt during the Civil War. It grew rapidly after 1900, as the role of the federal government in American life grew. It reached its population peak in 1950, with more than 800,000 people. Washington at that time was the eighth-largest city in the nation. Washington is now the fifteenth-largest city in the United States, as the population of the District of Columbia has continually shrunk since 1950. The population loss reflects the migration of residents to nearby Maryland and Virginia suburbs. Although the city itself may be losing population, the Washington metropolitan area (including the city and its suburbs) continues to gain population. More than 3 million people now live in the Washington metropolitan area. The list on the following page shows population growth in the District of Columbia since 1800.

Year	Population
1800	14,023
1820	33,039
1840	43,712
1860	75,080
1880	177,624
1900	278,718
1920	437,571
1940	663,091
1950	802,178
1960	763,956
1970	756,668
1980	638,432

GEOGRAPHY

Borders: Maryland borders the District of Columbia on the northwest, northeast, and southeast. The Potomac River forms the southwestern border, with Virginia on the other side of the Potomac.

Highest Point: Tenleytown, 410 ft. (125 m)

Lowest Point: Potomac River, 1 ft. (0.3 m)

Area: 69 sq. mi. (179 km²). The Washington metropolitan area measures 3,957 sq. mi. (10,249 km²). It includes Calvert, Charles, Frederick, Montgomery, and Prince Georges counties in Maryland; Arlington, Fairfax, Loudoun, Prince William, and Stafford counties in Virginia; and the Virginia cities of Alexandria, Fairfax, Falls Church, Manassas, and Manassas Park, which are not part of any county.

Rivers: Washington is located on the northeastern bank of the Potomac River, where the Anacostia River meets it from the northeast. At one time, the District occupied lands on both sides of the Potomac, but the southwestern part of the District was returned to Virginia in 1846. Rock Creek flows south from Maryland into the Potomac.

Lakes: Though no natural lakes lie within the District of Columbia, it nonetheless has well-known bodies of water. A lagoon called the Tidal Basin, which lies near the Jefferson Memorial, was created as a flood-control measure. The long Reflecting Pool separates the Washington Monument from the Lincoln Memorial. The Washington Channel lies between the heart of the District and East Potomac Park.

Topography: The District of Columbia lies within the Atlantic Coastal Plain, a low, flat area near the Atlantic Ocean. Rock Creek, in the northwest section, marks the boundary with the Piedmont, a broad plateau extending from Pennsylvania to Alabama.

Among the flowering trees that bloom in Washington during the spring are Japanese cherry trees (left) and dogwoods (above).

Climate: Members of Congress rush to leave the capital during their summer recess, and with good reason. Summers in Washington can be very uncomfortable. Temperatures in July range from 64° to 84° F. (18° to 29° C), but those temperatures combine with moist air to make a muggy climate. Temperatures are relatively mild in January—from 29° to 44° F. (-2° to 7° C). Most D.C. residents are not accustomed to heavy snow accumulation; a snowfall midwesterners might consider mild can tie up local traffic all day. Washingtonians did suffer under a 25-in. (64-cm) blizzard in January 1922. About 50 in. (127 cm) of precipitation falls annually. The highest recorded temperature was 106° F. (41° C) on July 30, 1930. The lowest recorded temperature was -15° F. (-26° C) on February 11, 1899.

NATURE

Trees: Sycamores, pin oaks, red oaks, American lindens, black walnuts, Japanese cherry trees, magnolias, dogwoods, ginkgos, Lombardy poplars, ailanthus, acacias, locusts

Wild Plants: Jack-in-the-pulpits, skunk cabbages, groundsels, Virginia bluebells, trailing arbutus, bloodroots, hepaticas

Animals: Squirrels, rabbits, raccoons, foxes, opossums, muskrats, flying squirrels

Birds: Sparrows, starlings, Baltimore orioles, warblers, thrushes, finches, mourning doves, chickadees, blue jays, mockingbirds

Fish: Shad, striped bass, largemouth bass, sunfish, pickerel, walleyed pike, catfish

GOVERNMENT

For nearly a century, District of Columbia residents had no say in their own local government. Some residents called the District "America's last colony." Congress gave the area some home rule as of 1974. But even now, Congress has the final say in District affairs. The budget, for example, once it is approved by the mayor and council, must be approved by Congress and the president.

A mayor and a thirteen-member council govern the city. All are elected to four-year terms. Five of the council members are elected at-large, the other eight from eight election districts. The mayor may veto council legislation, but the council may override the mayor's veto by a two-thirds vote.

District of Columbia residents elect a delegate to the House of Representatives. This delegate may serve on and vote in House committees but may not vote on final legislation. The Twenty-third Amendment to the Constitution gave D.C. residents the right to vote in presidential elections. The District has three electoral votes, the only area in which the electoral votes do not equal the number of its senators plus representatives.

Over the years, many District residents have sought increased self-government. In 1978, Congress approved a constitutional amendment that would allow D.C. two senators plus at least one representative in Congress. The amendment failed when it was not approved by legislatures in three-fourths of the states. Legislation regarding a 1982 movement for statehood under the name New Columbia is still pending in Congress.

U.S. Representatives: One nonvoting representative

Electoral Votes: 3

Voting Qualifications: United States citizen, eighteen years of age, registered to vote thirty days before an election

EDUCATION

Washington's public school system has about 185 schools with about 87,000 students. Another 25,000 or so students attend about 80 private schools. About 7,000 teachers serve District of Columbia students. Expenditure per public school student is about $3,500, a figure surpassed by only seven states.

The District has seventeen colleges and universities. The three-campus University of the District of Columbia, founded in 1976, is the only truly public school. Defense Intelligence College is another federally funded school. Howard University is famed as one of the nation's outstanding schools with a predominantly black enrollment. Gallaudet University attracts deaf and hearing-impaired students from around the world. Georgetown University is known for its strong foreign affairs department and nationally ranked basketball team. Other private schools in the nation's capital include American University, Catholic University, Corcoran School of Art, De Sales School of Theology, Dominican House

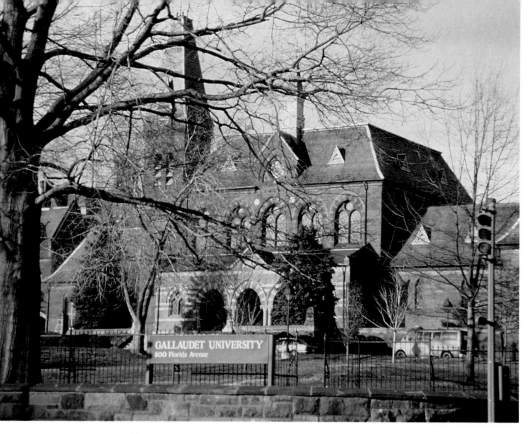

Gallaudet University attracts deaf and hearing-impaired students from around the world.

of Studies, George Washington University, Mount Vernon College, Oblate College, Southeastern University, Strayer College, Trinity College, and Wesley Theological Seminary.

ECONOMY AND INDUSTRY

Business and Trade: It is often said that Washington is a one-company town, and that company is the United States government. It is a valid claim. The elected officials, appointed officials, civil-service workers, lawyers, lobbyists, accountants, journalists, and service workers who cater to the above groups form most of the District of Columbia economic base. Tourism forms another important part of the economy, as many people work to serve the visitors who come to the capital on business or to see its magnificent sights.

George Washington, when he approved plans for the capital city, predicted that it would become a major commercial center. That vision went unfulfilled. Baltimore and Philadelphia remain the large nearby manufacturing and trade centers. The District of Columbia has no agriculture or mining. Printing and publishing provide the most important manufacturing industry. Food products, fabricated metals, and nonelectrical machinery provide a minor portion of the economy.

Transportation: Washington, as the nation's capital, naturally has good transportation links to cities everywhere in the country and to most of the rest of the world. Three major airports—Washington National, Baltimore-Washington

International, and Dulles International—serve air needs. Washington National handles about 6.5 million passengers each year, followed by Baltimore-Washington's 2.3 million and Dulles's 1.3 million.

The capital also serves as an important rail link. Amtrak trains leave each day to provide access to the heavily populated cities of the Northeast corridor and the Southeast. Five lines operate on about 50 mi. (80 km) of track. The District also has 1,517 mi. (2,441 km) of streets and roads. Perhaps the most important is Interstate 95, the Capital Beltway, which provides a route for thousands of Maryland and Virginia commuters.

A modern public transportation system serves Washington commuters. The Washington Area Metropolitan Transit Authority, or Metro, operates on about 50 mi. (80 km) of track, with plans to expand to about 100 mi. (161 km). A bus fleet claims about 171 million passenger trips each year.

Communication: The *Washington Post*, one of the largest newspapers in the nation, is also one of the most influential. It has produced many notable stories over the years. Its most famous moments came in the early 1970s, when two *Post* reporters unearthed events that led to the publicizing of the Watergate scandal. Another newspaper, the more conservative *Washington Times*, appears on weekday mornings. *USA Today*, a newspaper of nationwide circulation, originates near Washington. In addition, most important United States and foreign newspapers maintain permanent bureaus in the District of Columbia.

Many national magazines are published in Washington. These include the *National Review*, the *Smithsonian*, the *National Geographic*, *U.S. News & World Report*, *The Nation*, and *The New Republic*.

About twenty-three radio stations and eight television stations are located within the District. Residents may also tune into many other stations airing from nearby Baltimore, Philadelphia, or Virginia.

SOCIAL AND CULTURAL LIFE

Museums: James Smithson, a British citizen who never even saw the United States of America, earned a spot in the nation's heart. When he died in 1829, he bequeathed his entire fortune to the United States government "for the increase and diffusion of knowledge among men." The result of that generous gift was the Smithsonian Institution, a series of museums with more than 80 million objects in a dozen different buildings. A person looking at one object per second would need years to view all of the Smithsonian's holdings. The Smithsonian, which captures the American scientific, artistic, and cultural heritage with its many items, is sometimes referred to as the "nation's attic."

The Smithsonian contains a number of different museums and galleries. These include the National Museum of Natural History; the Arts and Industries Building, with its Victorian-era collection; the National Zoological Park; the Museum of African Art; Freer Gallery of Art, with the largest collection of Far and Near East items outside the Orient; the National Portrait Gallery; the National Gallery of Art; the Hirshhorn Museum and Sculpture Garden, with its large sculpture collection; and the National Museum of American Art, with more than twenty-six thousand items. The National Air and Space Museum, also part of the Smithsonian, is the most visited museum in the world.

Other, smaller museums honor everything from pharmacy to poultry to postage stamps. The Navy and Marine Corps each have museums displaying their heritage. The United States Naval Observatory houses a large telescope and exhibits. The Anacostia Neighborhood Museum focuses on black history. The Department of the Interior Museum shows national park exhibits and natural history. The National Geographic Society's Explorers Hall contains objects gathered from past expeditions sponsored by the society. The Textile Museum features rugs and textiles from Peru and the Near and Middle East. The Corcoran Gallery of Art houses American works from the beginning of the Republic, plus works by European masters. Other art museums include the Museum of Modern Art of Latin America, and the Phillips Collection, with its nineteenth- and twentieth-century art. Fort Ward Park Museum houses Civil War memorabilia. B'nai B'rith Klutznick Museum preserves Jewish culture.

Libraries: Washington, D.C., along with government departments in surrounding communities, contains more information than any other city on this planet. Of course, some of that information (such as diplomatic and military affairs) may never be made public. Even so, Washington libraries contain data that represent a substantial portion of the world's knowledge.

The Library of Congress, established in 1800, at first contained only about 3,000 books. When the British burned the capital in 1814, the fire destroyed that collection. Former president Thomas Jefferson sold his private library, which was more than twice the size of the original collection, to restart the library. Now it contains nearly 80 million items in three buildings, which are named after Presidents Thomas Jefferson, John Adams, and James Madison.

Washington would be a center of library research if it had nothing but the Library of Congress. But the nation's capital also boasts libraries from the many government and cultural groups that make their headquarters here, including the National Geographic Society, the National Genealogical Society, the United States Marine Corps, the Department of Health and Human Services, the National History Museum, the United States Naval Observatory, the John F. Kennedy Center for the Performing Arts, the United States Geological Survey, the American Institute of Pharmacy, and the Museum of African Art. The National Agricultural Library holds the most important collection of agricultural materials in the world. The Organization of American States Library contains information concerning the United States and Latin America. The Arthur D. Jenkins Library contains a large collection of textile literature. The Islamic Center contains thousands of volumes on Islamic culture. The District's fine public library — the Martin Luther King Memorial Library — has a Washingtoniana Division with a vast assortment of District of Columbia items. The Capitol Historical Society also has many volumes pertaining to the capital.

Performing Arts: Few artists of worldwide fame live in Washington or the surrounding communities. But almost every world-renowned artist has performed in the city. Many appear at the John Fitzgerald Kennedy Center for the Performing Arts, a magnificent cultural center that attracts the world's finest performing artists. The JFK Center houses an opera house, a concert hall, the Eisenhower

Theater, and the American Film Institute Theater. The American Ballet Theater and the National Symphony are among several nationally important institutions based in the JFK Center.

Even away from the Kennedy Center, the District of Columbia presents a wealth of musical, dance, and dramatic performances. The Corcoran Gallery hosts dance, chamber music, and theater performances. The Library of Congress holds many different concerts. The Dance Co-op and the Washington Project for the Arts are two of many dance centers. Christ Church holds concerts the first Sunday of each month. The Museum of African Art presents jazz, blues, and soul music. The Foundry, on the Chesapeake and Ohio Canal, is the site of many summertime folk and bluegrass performances. Wolf Trap Farm Park for the Performing Arts (in Vienna, Virginia), the only national park for the performing arts, hosts many musical and dramatic shows. Shakespeare and Company and the Atheneum are two of the many theaters presenting readings and full programs. Colleges and universities throughout the District offer plays and concerts. Bands and choruses from high schools, colleges, and churches throughout the nation give open-air concerts on the Capitol steps.

Sports and Recreation: Years ago, Washington had a baseball team known as the Senators. One of their players was Walter Johnson, perhaps the greatest pitcher ever to play. Unfortunately for the Senators, Johnson's teammates seldom matched his play. The Senators left Washington years ago. Baseball fans now travel to Baltimore and root for the Orioles, just as soccer fans visit Baltimore to cheer for the Blast. But Washingtonians cheer for football's Redskins. Basketball's Washington Bullets and hockey's Washington Capitals play their home games in nearby Landover, Maryland. Washingtonians enjoy the outdoors on many nearby golf and tennis courts. Some sail or fish in the Potomac River. Many stroll through or play in the local parks. Rock Creek Park, surrounding a creek that flows south from Maryland to the Potomac River, is the District of Columbia's largest park.

Historic Sites and Landmarks:

Arlington House (also known as the Custis-Lee Mansion), in Arlington, Virginia, was the home of Revolutionary statesman "Lighthorse Harry" Lee and Confederate Robert E. Lee.

Cedar Hill (the Frederick Douglass Home), at Fourteenth and W streets, was the first Washington house owned by the former slave who became an abolitionist, author, orator, journalist, and government official.

Chesapeake and Ohio Canal, parallel to the Potomac River through much of Georgetown, was America's first major canal and linked the Potomac River port of Georgetown with the nation's interior.

Congressional Cemetery, on the north bank of the Anacostia River in Northeast Washington, is the burial site of many senators, representatives, diplomats, military officers, and Cabinet members of the Republic's early years.

The pebble garden and pool at Dumbarton Oaks

Dumbarton Oaks, in Georgetown, was the site of the meeting of American, British, Russian, and Chinese officials that led to the formation of the United Nations.

Gadsby's Tavern, in Alexandria, Virginia, was an inn, a hostelry, and a gathering place for such early American leaders as George Washington, John Adams, Thomas Jefferson, James Monroe, Henry Clay, Francis Scott Key, Aaron Burr, and John Paul Jones.

Jefferson Memorial, overlooking the Tidal Basin, has a classical dome and is surrounded by twenty-six Ionic columns. It contains a statue of the third president of the United States.

Lincoln Memorial, facing the Reflecting Pool and the Washington Monument, contains a magnificent Daniel Chester French statue showing a contemplative, compassionate Abraham Lincoln.

Mount Vernon, in Mount Vernon, Virginia, was the plantation home of George Washington, the nation's first president.

Octagon House, facing Rawlins Square, served as the temporary home of President James Madison when the White House was being rebuilt after being burned by the British in 1814.

Ramsey House, in Alexandria, Virginia, is the oldest house in Alexandria and offers a film on the once-important tobacco port.

Red Cross Building, on Seventeenth Street south of the Corcoran Gallery of Art, is a shining white building with three beautiful Tiffany stained-glass windows that houses the national headquarters of the worldwide service organization.

St. John's Church, on Sixteenth Street, has served as a place of worship for every president since James Madison.

Stephen Decatur House, on Lafayette Square, home of the commodore who subdued the Barbary pirates, was the first private house built on this square.

Washington Monument, south of the White House, is the obelisk created to honor the nation's first president; it is the tallest structure in the District of Columbia and was the tallest structure on earth at the time of its completion.

Willard Hotel, on Pennsylvania Avenue, was a favorite meeting place of presidents such as Grant, Taft, Coolidge, Wilson, and Harding; it has been completely restored.

Woodrow Wilson House, on S Street, NW, was the last home of the twenty-eighth president, the only president who made his home in Washington after he retired.

Other Interesting Places to Visit:

Albert Einstein Memorial, on the grounds of the National Academy of Sciences, is a statue of the world-famous scientist that includes a precise map of the known universe at the time of the statue's 1979 dedication.

Arlington National Cemetery, in Arlington, Virginia, is the national cemetery for veterans and others, including Presidents William Howard Taft and John Fitzgerald Kennedy.

Blair House, on Pennsylvania Avenue near the White House, serves as official guest quarters for important visiting dignitaries; President Harry S. Truman lived there during a White House renovation.

Bureau of Engraving and Printing, on Fourteenth Street, SW, permits visitors to watch money being printed.

Capitol Building, on Capitol Hill, is the meeting place for Congress; the building contains a 180-ft.- (55-m-) high Rotunda, a Statuary Hall with statues honoring famous citizens from each state, and Senate and House wings; (the House wing is the largest legislative hall in the world).

Central Intelligence Agency, in Langley, Virginia, is the headquarters of America's international intelligence agency.

The Iwo Jima Statue, officially called the U.S. Marine Corps War Memorial (left), is located near Arlington National Cemetery (right).

Executive Office Building, at Pennsylvania Avenue and Seventeenth Street, patterned after the Louvre Museum in Paris, serves the White House staff and various government agencies.

Federal Bureau of Investigation, in the J. Edgar Hoover Building at Pennsylvania Avenue and Tenth Street, offers tours of the nation's law enforcement agency.

Ford's Theatre, on Tenth Street, NW, is the building in which President Abraham Lincoln was shot while watching the play *Our American Cousin.*

Gallaudet University, in Northeast Washington, is a famous college for the deaf.

Georgetown, in Northwest Washington, is a charming residential section of town that has beautiful homes in Federal and Victorian architectural styles as well as a lively strip of restaurants, art galleries, and boutiques.

Georgetown University, in Northwest Washington, is the oldest Roman Catholic college in the nation and contains one of the best-known schools for foreign service.

Government Printing Office, on North Capitol Street, is the world's largest printing complex.

Grant Memorial, at the western foot of Capitol Hill, is a group of statues that includes one of Civil War general and United States president Ulysses S. Grant— the largest equestrian statue in the nation and the second-largest in the world.

Howard University, in Northwest Washington, is America's largest black university.

Hubert H. Humphrey Building, near Capitol Hill, is a massive, modern structure that houses the Department of Health and Human Services.

Islamic Mosque and Cultural Center, on Massachusetts Avenue, NW, is a large white marble structure that serves as a mosque, a research facility, and an information center.

Iwo Jima Statue, near Arlington National Cemetery in Arlington, Virginia, is a bronze sculpture that was based on a famous photograph of Marines raising the American flag over Iwo Jima's Mount Suribachi; it is officially known as the U.S. Marine Corps War Memorial.

Kenilworth Aquatic Gardens, at Kenilworth Avenue and Douglas Street, NE, contain many ponds filled with colorful water plants.

National Arboretum, along the Anacostia River, protects hundreds of varieties of exotic trees and plants.

National Shrine of the Immaculate Conception, at Michigan Avenue and Fourth Street, NE, is the largest Roman Catholic church in the country.

National Zoological Park, in Rock Creek Park, is one of the finest zoos in the world, with some twenty-five hundred animals representing six hundred species.

Naval Hospital, in Bethesda, Maryland, is one of the nation's leading military hospitals.

Old Embassy Row, near Massachusetts Avenue and Twenty-third Street, has the greatest concentration of the many foreign embassies located in Washington.

The National Shrine of the Immaculate Conception is the largest Roman Catholic church in the country.

Old Post Office, south of the Mall in the Federal Triangle, is a Romanesque building with a 315-ft. (96-m) clock tower; it is now the site of the Pavilion, which contains shops, restaurants, and some government offices.

The Pentagon, near Arlington, Virginia, is one of the largest office buildings in the world; it houses the Department of Defense.

Smithsonian Institution Building, at the Mall near Eighth Street, is known as the Castle; the building housed the original museum but now serves as administration center for the vast Smithsonian complex.

Supreme Court Building, on First Street between East Capitol Street and Maryland Avenue, is a white marble building resembling a Greek temple that houses the highest court in the nation.

Tomb of the Unknowns, in Arlington National Cemetery, honors all Americans who died in the country's wars; it contains the bodies of four unidentified American soldiers—one who was killed during World War I, one during World War II, one during the Korean War, and one during the Vietnam War.

Treasury Building, just east of the White House, is a huge structure that is perhaps America's finest example of a Greek Revival building.

121

United States Botanic Garden, on Maryland Avenue at the western foot of Capitol Hill, displays more than ten thousand varieties of plants, including many rare species.

Vietnam Veterans Memorial, in Constitution Gardens between Constitution Avenue and the Reflecting Pool, is a V-shaped black granite monument with the names of all servicemen and servicewomen who perished or were declared missing in action during the Vietnam War; also part of the Memorial is a bronze statue of three soldiers—one white, one black, and one Hispanic.

Washington National Cathedral, at Wisconsin and Massachusetts avenues, is a stately Gothic structure that serves several denominations and is one of the largest religious buildings in the world.

Watergate Complex, on the Potomac River across from Theodore Roosevelt Island, is the shopping, residential, hotel, and office complex that was the site of the burglary that ultimately led to the resignation of President Richard Nixon.

White House, at 1600 Pennsylvania Avenue, NW, has been the home of every president since John Adams and is a world-famous symbol of the United States.

IMPORTANT DATES

1632—English fur trader Henry Fleete is the first European to live in the Washington area

1663—Duddington Manor, the largest tobacco estate within the present-day District of Columbia, begins operation

1680—Piscataway Indians abandon their villages in the present District of Columbia region

1749—Settlers found Alexandria, Virginia, the first town in the area

1751—Maryland colonists found the trading port of Georgetown

1783—The Treaty of Paris grants American independence

1787—The United States Constitution provides that a tract of land be reserved for the federal government

1789—French military engineer Pierre-Charles L'Enfant asks to be appointed the designer of the "capital of this vast empire"

1790—Congress authorizes President Washington to choose a site along the Potomac River for the future capital

1791—Washington appoints Andrew Ellicott to survey the area and hires French military engineer L'Enfant to draw up plans for a federal city

1792—Construction begins on the White House, then referred to as the Presidential Palace

1800—The District of Columbia becomes the nation's capital; John Adams becomes the first president to occupy the White House

1802—The city of Washington is incorporated

1814—British forces invade and burn the Capitol and other Washington buildings

1819—Reconstruction is completed on the Capitol and the White House

1828—The Chesapeake and Ohio Canal links the District of Columbia with the lands beyond the Allegheny Mountains

1829—Englishman James Smithson leaves his vast fortune to the United States "to found in Washington, under the name Smithsonian Institution, an establishment for the increase and diffusion of knowledge among men"

1846—The District cedes the Virginia portion of its land back to Virginia on the assumption that the federal government would not need the land; an act of Congress creates the Smithsonian Institution

1848—Construction begins on the Washington Monument

1850—The Compromise of 1850 outlaws slave trade in the District of Columbia

1852—The Smithsonian Institution opens

1861—The Seventh Regiment from New York enters Washington, guaranteeing that the capital would not fall to the Confederates during the Civil War; troops march from Washington to fight Confederate troops at nearby Bull Run, followed by Washingtonian civilians wishing to see an easy Union victory, but well-prepared Confederate troops rout the Union soldiers

1865—Southern sympathizer John Wilkes Booth assassinates President Abraham Lincoln

1867—The United States Freedmen's Bureau establishes Howard University

1871—Congress creates a territorial form of government for the District; Georgetown merges with Washington

1874—Congress abolishes the territorial government because of alleged local extravagances, and establishes a system of three commissioners, each appointed by the president

1881 — A disappointed office seeker assassinates President James A. Garfield at the Baltimore and Potomac Railway station

1885 — The Washington Monument is completed

1926 — The United States Supreme Court upholds the law forbidding black or Jewish people to move into many District neighborhoods

1929 — The Great Depression brings massive unemployment to the District of Columbia

1932 — Thousands of unemployed World War I veterans known as the "bonus marchers" demonstrate in the capital; President Herbert Hoover orders the United States Army to evict them

1935 — The Supreme Court building is completed

1939 — Marian Anderson, a black opera star, sings before thousands at the Lincoln Memorial after being denied the chance to sing at a concert in Constitution Hall because of her race

1944 — Delegates from the United States, Great Britain, Russia, and China meet at Dumbarton Oaks to plan an organization that would seek to prevent future wars

1948 — President Harry S. Truman moves into Blair House while the White House undergoes renovation

1950 — Puerto Rican nationalists attempt to assassinate President Truman; Washington's population peaks at more than 800,000

1961 — The Twenty-third Amendment permits D.C. residents to vote in presidential elections

1963 — Dr. Martin Luther King, Jr., leads 200,000 demonstrators in Washington civil-rights demonstration and makes his famous "I have a dream" speech; President John F. Kennedy is assassinated and laid to rest in Arlington National Cemetery

1964 — The Museum of African Art and the Douglass Institute of Negro Arts and History opens, the first American museum devoted exclusively to African art

1965 — President Lyndon Johnson introduces an unsuccessful bill to give the District of Columbia home rule

1967 — Washington native Edward Albee wins the Pulitzer Prize in drama for *A Delicate Balance*

1968 — A riot following the assassination of Dr. Martin Luther King, Jr., claims nine lives

1970—The District of Columbia is allowed to send nonvoting delegates to the House of Representatives

1972—Burglars break into Democratic National Committee headquarters at the Watergate apartment and office complex, setting off a scandal that ultimately forces President Richard Nixon to resign from office

1973—Congress provides the District of Columbia with a home-rule charter

1975—An elected mayor and city council take office; Edward Albee wins a Pulitzer Prize in drama for *Seascape*

1980—Washingtonians vote to apply for statehood

1981—A would-be assassin's bullet nearly kills President Ronald Reagan

1982—Forty-five delegates draft a constitution for the proposed state of New Columbia, but Congress fails to act on the request; Art Buchwald wins a Pulitzer Prize for commentary

IMPORTANT PEOPLE

Cleveland Abbe (1838-1916), meteorologist; helped develop the U.S. Weather Service (1870); served as meteorologist when U.S. Weather Bureau was established (1871-1916); taught at Columbian College (now George Washington University); helped to establish standard time for the entire world

Robert Abernathy (1927-   ), journalist; grew up in Washington; served for years as reporter and occasional anchor with NBC news; covered Washington politics, science, and education; wrote *Introduction to Tomorrow*, an award-winning history book for teenagers

CLEVELAND ABBE

EDWARD ALBEE

ELGIN BAYLOR

ALEXANDER GRAHAM BELL

EMILE BERLINER

Henry Brooks Adams (1838-1918), writer and historian; settled in Washington in 1877; best known for his novel *Democracy* and his autobiography, *The Education of Henry Adams*

Edward Albee (1928-   ), born in Washington; dramatist; many of his plays, which deal with both realism and fancy, were influenced by the absurdist movement; gained fame with *Who's Afraid of Virginia Woolf?*; received Pulitzer Prizes in drama for *A Delicate Balance* (1967) and *Seascape* (1975)

Bailey Kelly Ashford (1873-1934), born in Washington; soldier and surgeon; discovered and helped eradicate hookworm, a parasite that caused tropical anemia in Puerto Rico

Benjamin Banneker (1731-1806), astronomer, mathematician, and surveyor; assisted Andrew Ellicott in his surveys of the District of Columbia; published a yearly almanac (1791-96); constructed a working clock, its pieces made entirely of wood, without ever having seen a clock

Marion Shepilov Barry, Jr. (1936-   ), politician; mayor of Washington (1978-   ); oversaw downtown area renewal; underwent a number of scandals in his later terms

Clara Barton (1821-1892), nurse; tended to the wounded in Washington during the Civil War, becoming known as the Angel of the Battlefield and Lady with the Lamp; organized the American Red Cross; wrote *The Red Cross* and *A Story of the Red Cross*

Samuel Adrian Baugh (1914-   ), professional football player; a strong-armed quarterback known as "Slingin' Sammy" who propelled the Washington Redskins to titles in the early 1940s; held every NFL game, season, and career passing record at one time; member of the Pro Football Hall of Fame (1963)

Elgin Baylor (1934-   ), born in Washington; professional basketball player; starred with the Minneapolis and Los Angeles Lakers as one of the game's greatest forwards

Alexander Graham Bell (1847-1922), inventor; moved to Washington in 1879; invented the telephone; patented the gramophone and wax recording cylinders; president of the National Geographic Society (1896-1904)

Deane Beman (1938-   ), born in Washington; golfer; had one of the best amateur records in late 1950s and early 1960s; won both American and British amateur events; won four PGA tour events; PGA Tour Commissioner (1974-   )

Emile Berliner (1851-1929), born in Washington; inventor; designed a practical telephone transmitter; invented a way to cut phonograph records from a master disc

Carl Bernstein (1944-   ), born in Washington; journalist; worked with Robert Woodward for the *Washington Post* to expose the Watergate scandal; wrote *All the President's Men*

David Brinkley (1920-   ), journalist and commentator; pioneered television news broadcasting with NBC's "Huntley-Brinkley Report" and "David Brinkley's Journal"; hosted "This Week with David Brinkley" on ABC; wrote *Washington During the War*, a book describing how the capital city dealt with World War II

DAVID BRINKLEY

Edward Brooke (1919-   ), born in Washington; politician; awarded the Bronze Star for bravery in World War II; became the first black U.S. senator since Reconstruction; senator from Massachusetts (1967-79)

Art Buchwald (1925-   ), resident of Washington; columnist, humorist; specializes in political and social satire; received the Pulitzer Prize for commentary (1982); published several books of collections from his newspaper columns

Billie Burke (1886-1970), born Mary William Ethelbert Appleton Burke in Washington; actress and author; played fluttery movie roles, including the good witch Glinda in *The Wizard of Oz*; wrote two autobiographies: *With a Feather on My Nose* and *With Powder on My Nose*

BILLIE BURKE

Frances Hodgson Burnett (1849-1924), novelist and playwright; spent several years in Washington; best known as author of the children's books *Little Lord Fauntleroy* and *The Secret Garden*

Marshall Whiting Cassidy (1892-1968), born in Washington; Thoroughbred racing official; worked as a steward, starter, timer, judge, racing secretary, racing director, and racetrack designer; pioneered the mechanical-stall starting gate now used for most horse races; perfected the photo-finish camera

Connie Chung (1946-   ), born in Washington; journalist; reported and anchored newscasts for CBS and NBC; hosted "News at Sunrise" and "Saturday Night with Connie Chung"

CONNIE CHUNG

Ina Clare (1892-   ), born Ina Fagan in Washington; actress and vaudeville comedienne; appeared in many silent films and on Broadway stage; played bubbly roles and sophisticated comedy; starred in *Ninotchka*

Benjamin Oliver Davis (1877-1970), born in Washington; U.S. Army officer; became the first black general in the army (1940); served in Liberia, Mexico, the Philippines and in the Spanish-American War; helped desegregate the armed forces in World War II

Benjamin Oliver Davis, Jr. (1912-   ), born in Washington; U.S. Air Force officer; became the first black general in the Air Force in 1965; earned the Distinguished Flying Cross in World War II; served as assistant secretary of transportation (1971-75)

BENJAMIN O. DAVIS, JR.

CHARLES DREW

JOHN FOSTER DULLES

DUKE ELLINGTON

EDWARD GALLAUDET

Charles Richard Drew (1904-1950), born in Washington; physician; researched the uses of blood plasma; set up many blood banks; convinced doctors to use plasma for emergency operations; professor, Howard University (1945-50); received the Spingarn Medal (1944)

John Foster Dulles (1888-1959), born in Washington; statesman; negotiated the Japanese peace treaty (1949-51); helped form United Nations (1944-45); U.N. delegate (1946-49); U.S. secretary of state (1953-59); as secretary of state, took hard line against communism

Andrew Ellicott (1754-1820), surveyor; helped lay out the design for the capital; succeeded Pierre-Charles L'Enfant and made some minor changes in L'Enfant's designs

Duke Ellington (1899-1974), born Edward Kennedy Ellington in Washington; jazz composer and pianist; ranked among the giants in the history of jazz; composed extended jazz works that highlighted individual instruments; composed "Sophisticated Lady" and "Mood Indigo"; among his major compositions was "Black, Brown, and Beige," a tonal history of black people in America

Walter Edward Fauntroy (1933-   ), born in Washington; politician; helped secure limited home rule for the District of Columbia (1973)

Edward Miner Gallaudet (1837-1917), educator; founded Gallaudet University, the first institution of higher learning for the deaf in the United States

Henry Gannett (1846-1914), geographer and cartographer; founded the Geological Society of America; a founder and president of the National Geographic Society (1888)

Marvin Gaye (1939-1984), born in Washington; singer and songwriter; known for his soulful songs; recorded "I Heard It through the Grapevine," the best-selling song in the history of Motown Records; scored hits with "How Sweet It Is," "Ain't No Mountain High Enough," and "What's Going On"

Leon Allen "Goose" Goslin (1900-1971), professional baseball player; his batting average was .316 over an eighteen-year career; slugged seven home runs for the Washington Senators in three World Series; member of the Baseball Hall of Fame (1968)

Katharine Graham (1917-   ), born Katharine Meyer; publisher; chairman of the board of the *Washington Post*, affiliated television and radio stations, and *Newsweek* magazine; encouraged the investigation that led to the uncovering of the Watergate scandal

Clark Calvin Griffith (1869-1955), professional baseball player and executive; helped organize baseball's American League; led the Chicago White Sox to the first A.L. pennant (1901); played for, managed, and owned the Washington Senators for more than four decades; member of the Baseball Hall of Fame (1946)

Gilbert Hovey Grosvenor (1875-1966), geographer; edited the *National Geographic* magazine (1899-1954); director (1899-1966), president (1920-54), chairman of the board (1954-66) of the National Geographic Society

CLARK GRIFFITH

Stanley Raymond "Bucky" Harris (1896-1977), professional baseball player and manager; Washington Senators' second baseman for ten years; managed the Senators to the team's first two pennants (1924, 1925); member of the Baseball Hall of Fame (1975)

Patricia Roberts Harris (1924-1985), lawyer and political official; on faculty of Howard University law school (1961-70), dean (1969-70); became the first black woman to serve as a director of a major company (IBM, 1971); the first black woman to hold a Cabinet post; secretary of Housing and Urban Development (1977-79); secretary of Health, Education, and Welfare (1979); secretary of Health and Human Services (1979-81)

GILBERT GROSVENOR

Goldie Hawn (1945-   ), born in Washington; actress; member of the cast of the television show "Rowan and Martin's Laugh-In"; won an Academy Award as best supporting actress for *Cactus Flower* (1969); starred in the movies *Private Benjamin*, *There's a Girl in My Soup*, and *Butterflies Are Free*

Helen Hayes (1900-   ), born Helen Hayes Brown in Washington; actress; called the "First Lady of the American Theater"; won Academy Awards as best actress in *Sin of Madelon Claudet* (1931) and as best supporting actress in *Airport* (1970); appeared on Broadway for decades, in productions such as *Victoria Regina* and *Dear Brutus*; wrote an autobiography, *On Reflection*

PATRICIA HARRIS

Robert Hooks (1937-   ), born in Washington; actor and producer; cofounded the Negro Ensemble Company, a New York repertory company; earned a reputation for versatility on the Broadway stage in productions such as *A Taste of Honey*, *The Milk Train Doesn't Stop Here Anymore*, and *Where's Daddy?*

John (J.) Edgar Hoover (1895-1972), born in Washington; government official; director, Federal Bureau of Investigation (1924-72); reformed the FBI, established the world's largest fingerprint file, and developed a crime laboratory; tracked down many well-known criminals but was accused at times of civil-rights violations

ROBERT HOOKS

OLIVER OTIS HOWARD

MICHAEL LEARNED

ALICE R. LONGWORTH

GEORGE MARSHALL

Oliver Otis Howard (1830-1909), soldier and educator; Civil War general; director of the Freedmen's Bureau (1865-74); founded Howard University (1867), president (1869-74); superintendent of West Point (1881-82)

Jesse Jackson (1941-   ), activist, minister, and political leader; founded Operation PUSH; ran for president in 1984 and 1988, winning many primary votes but losing the Democratic nomination both times; maintains a residence in Washington and has contemplated running for D.C. mayor

Walter Perry Johnson (1887-1946), professional baseball player; was considered by many the greatest pitcher who ever lived; won 416 games for the Washington Senators; led the American League in wins six times and strikeouts twelve times; holds the major-league record with 110 shutouts; led the Senators to two pennants (1924, 1925) and one World Series win (1924); member of the Baseball Hall of Fame (1936)

John Paul Jones (1890-1970), born in Washington; athlete; held the first official amateur record for the mile; ran 4:04.4 in 1913; set many long-distance racing records at Cornell University; finished fourth in the 1500-meter race in the 1912 Olympics

Harmon Clayton Killebrew (1936-   ), professional baseball player; led the American League with 42 home runs for the 1959 Washington Senators; led the A.L. in home runs six times; hit 573 career homers, fifth on the all-time list; member of the Baseball Hall of Fame (1984)

Benjamin Henry Latrobe (1764-1820), architect; completed the south wing of the U.S. Capitol; directed much of the reconstruction of D.C. after the British destruction during the War of 1812

Michael Learned (1939-   ), born in Washington; actress; appeared in such television dramas as "The Waltons" and "Nurse"

Pierre-Charles L'Enfant (1754-1825), engineer; became the first city planner in the United States; prepared a plan for a new U.S. capital city in the District of Columbia; conceived parks, public buildings, and wide, radiating streets; designed Federal Hall in New York City

Alice Roosevelt Longworth (1884-1980), socialite; conversed with every president from Benjamin Harrison to Gerald Ford; inspired the song "Alice Blue Gown" when her father, Theodore Roosevelt, was in the White House; acted as unofficial queen of Washington social activities from her father's time to her death

George Preston Marshall (1896-1969), football executive; moved the failing Boston Redskins franchise to Washington and made it one of the sport's most successful teams; a charter member of the Pro Football Hall of Fame (1963)

Graham McNamee (1888-1942), born in Washington; sportscaster; became known as the first great radio sports announcer; covered the first World Series (1923) and the first political convention (Democratic, 1924) to be broadcast; covered Charles Lindbergh's return to Washington and Admiral Byrd's return from the South Pole

Roger Mudd (1928-), born in Washington; journalist; reporter and anchorman for CBS and NBC; has a reputation for knowledge of political affairs in the capital city

ROGER MUDD

Eleanor Holmes Norton (1937-), born in Washington; lawyer, government official; became the first woman chairman of the New York City Commission on Human Rights; specialized in cases involving freedom of speech; formed the National Black Feminist Organization; advocated tough anti-blockbusting legislation; professor of law at Georgetown University (1982-)

Hildy Parks (1926-), born in Washington; writer, actress, and producer; produced the annual television broadcast of the Tony awards; won two Emmy awards, one for a Tony awards program and one for "Night of 100 Stars"

LEONARD ROSE

Edgar Charles "Sam" Rice (1890-1974), professional baseball player; cracked more than 2,900 hits for the Washington Senators; retired with a .322 lifetime batting average; led the Senators to three pennants and the 1924 World Series title; member of the Baseball Hall of Fame (1963)

Chita Rivera (1933-), born Dolores Conchita Figuero del Rivero in Washington; dancer, actress, and singer; starred in Broadway musicals such as *West Side Story*, *Bye, Bye Birdie*, and *The Rink*; won a Tony award for *The Rink* (1984)

Leonard Rose (1918-1984), born in Washington; cellist; performed with a technique many critics described as flawless; played with Cleveland and New York City symphony orchestras; taught at the Julliard School of Music

MARK RUSSELL

Mark Russell (1932-), born Mark Ruslander; humorist; lives in Washington; plays piano while reciting jokes and singing songs satirizing Washington, D.C., and government officials; appears on television, radio, and on stage; pokes fun at both Democrats and Republicans

Antonin Scalia (1936-), jurist; member of the U.S. Court of Appeals from the District of Columbia (1982-86); associate justice of the U.S. Supreme Court (1986-), the first American of Italian descent appointed to the court

Frank Gill Slaughter (1908-), born in Washington; physician and author; wrote novels about the medical profession, including *Spencer Brade, M.D.* and *That None Shall Die*

ANTONIN SCALIA

JOHN PHILIP SOUSA

WILLIAM THORNTON

ROBERT WEAVER

John Philip Sousa (1854-1932), born in Washington; composer known as the "March King"; wrote "The Stars and Stripes Forever," a favorite Fourth of July march; composed more than one hundred marches, including "Semper Fidelis" and "The Washington Post"; led the U.S. Marine Band (1880-92); bandmaster for the U.S. Navy (1917-19)

William Thornton (1759-1828), physician; submitted the winning design for the Capitol; persuaded the British not to burn records of the federal patent office; designed Octagon House

Peter Tork (1944-   ), born in Washington; actor and singer; starred as a band member in the television series "The Monkees"

George Washington (1732-1799), first president of the United States (1789-97); commanded colonial forces to victory over England in the Revolutionary War; as president, assigned and approved plans for a federal district to become the nation's capital

Walter Edward Washington (1915-   ), politician; became the first black chief executive of a major American city as District of Columbia commissioner (1967-75); became the first modern mayor of Washington (1975-79)

Robert Weaver (1907-   ), born in Washington; government official; as secretary of Housing and Urban Development (1966-68) was the first black person to attain Cabinet status; president of Bernard M. Baruch College (1969-70); chairman, NAACP (1978-   )

Woodrow Wilson (1856-1924), twenty-eighth president of the United States (1913-21); tried to keep the United States out of World War I; awarded the 1920 Nobel Peace Prize for his work to establish League of Nations; lived in Washington after his presidency, the only former president to remain in the capital after his retirement

William V. "Willie" Wood (1936-   ), born in Washington; professional football player; played with colorful verve as a punt returner and defensive back for the great Green Bay Packer teams of the 1960s; led the Packers to five NFL titles, including two Super Bowls; member of the Pro Football Hall of Fame (1989)

MAYORS

Walter Washington	1975-1979
Marion Barry	1979-

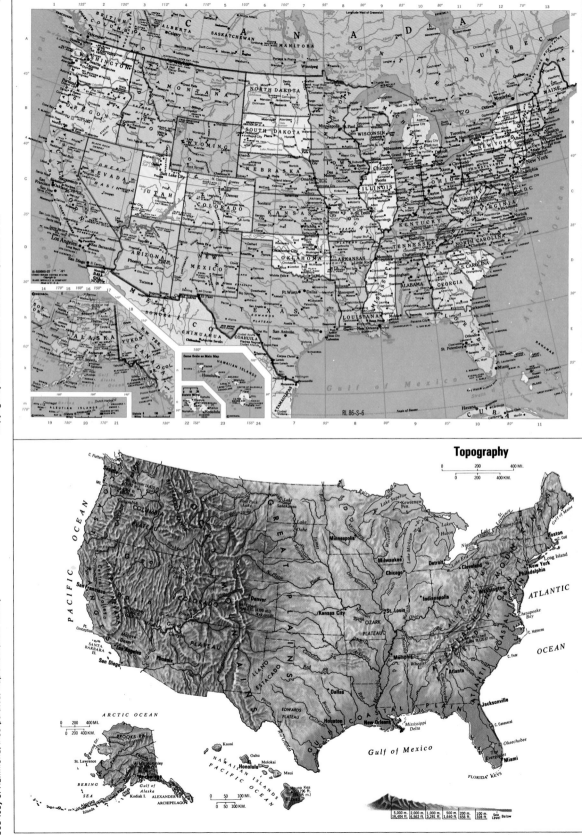

Topography

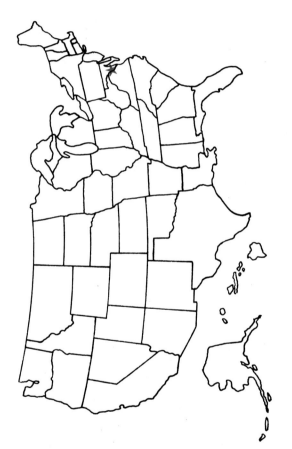

50. National Historical Wax Museum — A5
51. National Museum of Natural History — C4
52. National Portrait Gallery — B5
53. Octagon House — B3
54. Organization of American States — B4
55. Pentagon (Department of Defense) — E2
56. Petersen House — B4
57. Postal Service — B4
58. Reflecting Pool — C3
59. Robert A. Taft Memorial — B6
60. Senate Office Buildings — B6
61. Smithsonian Institution Building — C4
62. State, Department of — B3
63. Supreme Court — C6
64. Theodore Roosevelt Memorial — B2
65. Tomb of the Unknowns — D1
66. Transportation, Department of — C5
67. Treasury Building — B4
68. Union Station — B6
69. United States Botanic Garden — C6
70. United States Weather Bureau — A3
71. Washington Monument — C4
72. Washington Navy Yard — D7
73. Watergate Complex — B2
74. White House — B4
75. World Bank — B3

24. Government Printing Office — B6
25. Health and Human Services, Department of — C5
26. Hirshhorn Museum and Sculpture Garden — C6
27. House Office Buildings — C5
28. Housing and Urban Development, Department of — B3
29. Interior, Department of the — B4
30. Internal Revenue Building — B4
31. Jefferson Memorial — D4
32. John F. Kennedy Center for the Performing Arts — B2
33. John F. Kennedy Eternal Flame — D1
34. Judiciary Square — B5
35. Justice, Department of — B5
36. Labor, Department of — B4
37. Lafayette Square — B4
38. L'Enfant Plaza — C5
39. Library of Congress — C6
40. Lincoln Memorial — C3
41. Marine Corps War Memorial — C1
42. Martin Luther King Memorial Library — B5
43. Museum of African Art — C6
44. Museum of American History, National — C4
45. National Academy of Sciences — B3
46. National Aeronautics and Space Administration — C5
47. National Air and Space Museum — C5
48. National Archives — B5
49. National Gallery of Art — C5

MAP KEY

1. Agriculture, Department of — C4
2. American Red Cross Headquarters — B3
3. Arts and Industries Building — C5
4. Blair House — B4
5. Bureau of Engraving and Printing — C4
6. Capitol — C6
7. Chesapeake and Ohio Canal — A2
8. Commerce, Department of — B4
9. Constitution Hall — B4
10. Corcoran Gallery of Art — B4
11. Custis-Lee Mansion (Arlington House) — D1
12. Ellipse — B4
13. Executive Office Building — B3
14. Federal Bureau of Investigation (J. Edgar Hoover Building) — B5
15. Federal Reserve Board — B3
16. Federal Trade Commission — B5
17. Folger Shakespeare Library — C6
18. Ford's Theatre — B5
19. Fort Lesley J. McNair — E5
20. Fort Meyer — D1
21. Freer Gallery of Art — C4
22. George Washington University — B3
23. Georgetown University — A1

Reprinted with permission of *The New Book of Knowledge,* © Grolier Inc.

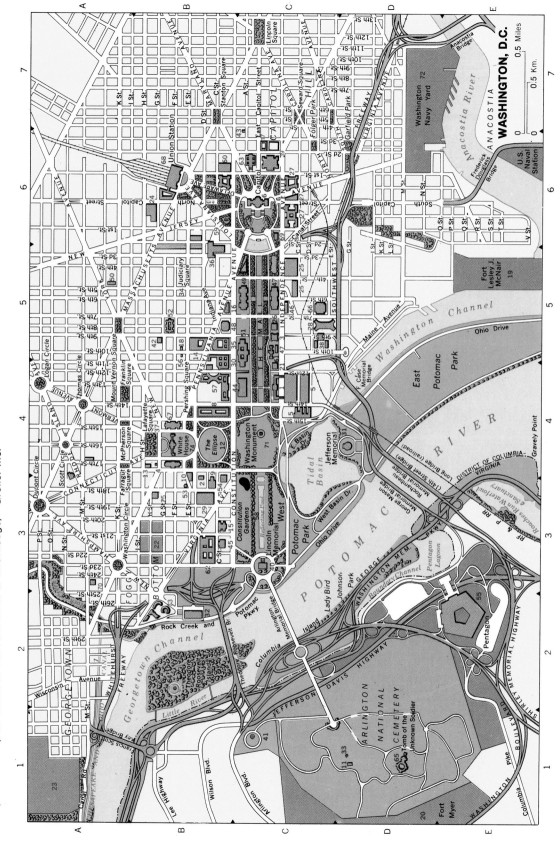

WASHINGTON, D.C.

Restored homes line the Chesapeake & Ohio Canal in Georgetown.

INDEX

Page numbers that appear in boldface type indicate illustrations

Each year, thousands of Vietnam survivors, as well as parents, widows, children, and friends of those who died, make the pilgrimage to the beautiful and moving Vietnam Veterans Memorial.

Picture Identifications

Front cover: An evening view of Washington
Back cover: The Jefferson Memorial
Pages 2-3: The Washington Monument
Page 6: A mother and child at the Lincoln Memorial
Pages 8-9: The Washington Monument from the Tidal Basin
Pages 16-17: A montage of Washingtonians
Pages 22-23: Washington as it looked in 1800
Pages 36-37: A view of the White House as it looked in 1877
Page 52: The interior of Union Station, after restoration
Page 64: A view of Georgetown, with Georgetown University in the background
Page 70: The rotunda of the Museum of Natural History
Pages 80-81: A view of Washington at sunset, showing the lighted monuments
Page 92: The statue of Lincoln in the Lincoln Memorial
Page 108: A montage showing the District flag, the District tree (scarlet oak), the District bird (wood thrush), and the District flower (American beauty rose)

About the Author

Deborah Kent grew up in Little Falls, New Jersey, and received a Bachelor of Arts degree in English from Oberlin College. She earned a Masters degree in Social Work from Smith College School for Social Work, and worked for four years at the University Settlement House on New York's Lower East Side. She later moved to San Miguel de Allende, Mexico, where she began to write full time.

Deborah Kent has published a dozen novels for young adults, as well as numerous titles in the *America the Beautiful* series. She lives in Chicago with her husband and their daughter Janna.

Picture Acknowledgments

Front cover, © William R. Kulik/**Photri;** 2-3, © Dave Gess/**Third Coast Stock Source;** 4, © **Cameramann International, Ltd.;** 5, © R. Krubner/**H. Armstrong Roberts;** 6, © Jake McGuire/**Washington Stock Photo;** 8-9, © **Gene Ahrens;** 11, **Shostal/SuperStock;** 12, © Jake McGuire/**Washington Stock Photo;** 13, © Robert S. Scurlock/**Shostal/SuperStock;** 14 (left), © Glenn Jahnke/**Root Resources;** 14 (right), **H. Armstrong Roberts;** 16 (top), © M. S. Valada/**Folio Inc.;** 16 (bottom left), © Lloyd Wolf/**Folio Inc.;** 16 (bottom right), **Photri;** 17 (top left), © Carl Purcell/**Words and Pictures;** 17 (top right), © Everett C. Johnson/**Folio Inc.;** 17 (bottom left), © Jake McGuire/ **Washington Stock Photo;** 17 (bottom right), **Photri;** 19, © Jim Pickerell/**TSW-Click/Chicago Ltd.;** 20 (left), **Photri,** 20 (right), © Skip Brown/**Folio Inc.;** 21, © Skip Brown/**Folio Inc.;** 22-23, **North Wind Picture Archives;** 25, **North Wind Picture Archives;** 28 (left), **Library of Congress;** 28 (right), **North Wind Picture Archives;** 29, **Photri;** 31 (top), **Maryland Historical Society;** 31 (middle and bottom), **Library of Congress;** 32, **The Bettmann Archive;** 34, **Photri;** 35, **North Wind Picture Archives;** 36-37, **North Wind Picture Archives;** 39, **The New York Public Library, Phelps Stokes Collection;** 41, **The Bettmann Archive;** 42, **Photri;** 43, © Camerique/**H. Armstrong Roberts;** 45, **The Bettmann Archive;** 46 (both pictures), **The Bettmann Archive;** 49 (both pictures), **Photri;** 50, **Photri;** 52, © R. Krubner/**H. Armstrong Roberts;** 54, **AP/Wide World Photos;** 57, **AP/Wide World Photos;** 58, **AP/Wide World Photos;** 60 (left), **AP/Wide World Photos;** 60 (right), © **Cameramann International, Ltd.;** 62, **AP/Wide World Photos;** 63, © R. Krubner/**H. Armstrong Roberts;** 64, © B. Kulik/**Photri;** 66 (both pictures), **Photri;** 67, © Pete Saloutos/**TSW-Click/Chicago Ltd.;** 68, © Lani/**Photri;** 69, © **Cameramann International, Ltd.;** 70, © Tim McCabe/**Journalism Services;** 72 (both pictures), **North Wind Picture Archives;** 74, **Photri;** 75 (left), **Photri;** 75 (right), © **Tom Dietrich;** 77, **Shostal/SuperStock;** 78, **Photri;** 79, **Photri;** 80-81, © Mark Segal/**TSW-Click/ Chicago Ltd.;** 83 (left), © Paul F. Gero/**Journalism Services;** 83 (right), © Jake McGuire/**Washington Stock Photo;** 84 (left), reprinted with permission of *The New Book of Knowledge,* © **Grolier Inc.;** 84 (right), **Photri;** 85, **Photri;** 86, **Photri;** 87, © Lani/**Photri;** 88, **Shostal/SuperStock;** 89, **Photri;** 91, © J. Novak/**Photri;** 92, **Photri;** 94 (left), **H. Armstrong Roberts;** 94 (right), **Photri;** 95 (both pictures), **Photri;** 96 (left), **Shostal/SuperStock;** 96 (right), **H. Armstrong Roberts;** 97, **Photri;** 98, © David M. Doody/**Tom Stack & Associates;** 100, **SuperStock;** 102 (top left and top right), **Shostal/SuperStock;** 102 (bottom left), © Jake McGuire/**Washington Stock Photo;** 102 (bottom right), © Tim McCabe/ **Journalism Services;** 105, © **Tom Dietrich;** 106 (left), © Sam Saylor/**Greenberg;** 106 (right), © Tim McCabe/**Journalism Services;** 107 (right), © Matthew Kaplan/**Marilyn Gartman Agency;** 108 (background), © **Norma Morrison;** 108 (rose), © V. Bider/**Photri;** 108 (bird), © Helen Kittinger/**Photo Options;** 108 (flag), **Courtesy Flag Research Center, Winchester, Massachusetts 01890;** 111 (left), © **Gene Ahrens;** 111 (right), **Photri;** 113, **Photri;** 117, **Photri;** 119 (left), © Raymond Prucha/**Root Resources;** 119 (right), © D. Corson/**H. Armstrong Roberts;** 121, © Robert S. Scurlock/**Shostal/SuperStock;** 125, **Historical Pictures Service, Chicago;** 126 (all four pictures), **AP/Wide World Photos;** 127 (all four pictures), **AP/Wide World Photos;** 128 (Drew, Dulles, Ellington), **AP/Wide World Photos;** 128 (Gallaudet), **Historical Pictures Service, Chicago;** 129 (all four pictures), **AP/Wide World Photos;** 130 (Howard), **North Wind Picture Archives;** 130 (Learned, Longworth, Marshall), **AP/Wide World Photos;** 131 (all four pictures), **AP/Wide World Photos;** 132 (Sousa), **AP/Wide World Photos;** 132 (Thornton, Weaver), **Historical Pictures Service, Chicago;** 136, © T. Dietrich/**H. Armstrong Roberts;** 139, © Ed Kreminski/**Third Coast Stock Source;** back cover, © Bob Glander/**Shostal/SuperStock**